The Pinchot Impact Index

Measuring, Comparing, and Aggregating Impact

by Michael "Luni" Libes

Revision 1.0

ISBN-10: 0692396519
ISBN-13: 978-0692396513

Introduction

This book provides a new solution on how to **measure, compare** and **aggregate** the impact of organizations that aim to do good in the world.

Measure: How do you measure the impact of a nonprofit, for-profit, or government organization?

Compare: How do you compare the impacts of two projects, within or between two organizations?

Aggregate: How do you sum up the impact of two or more disparate projects?

These are difficult questions which organizations have struggled to answer for decades.

Before jumping into the proposed solution, the book first clarifies the issues of measuring, comparing and aggregating impact, and describes the current state of the art answers to these questions. Concrete examples demonstrate problems still unsolved by those answers.

The next section introduces the mathematical concept of **orders of magnitude**. You learned the basics of this back in grammar school when learning how to count. Orders of magnitude is a key component in the proposed new index.

Finally, the book concludes with the proposed solution: the **Pinchot Impact Index**. This section dives deeply into how the Pinchot Impact Index works, where it works, and the implications of this solution.

Inspiration

This index and its approach to measuring, comparing, and aggregating impact was inspired by a conversation with Gifford Pinchot III at what was then called the Bainbridge Graduate Institute (BGI), where I volunteer and teach.

Gifford was attempting to describe the difference in happiness between enjoying a round of traditional golf (with all of its negative environmental repercussions) vs. enjoying round of Frisbee golf in the woods at his off-the-grid eco-friendly island retreat. BGI teaches "Sustainable Business" and so such conversations are quite normal at this unique "business school in the woods".

Comparing forms of golf is a paradigm example for Gifford's *Happo Dammo Ratio*, a ratio of happiness vs. environmental damage. In working through the issues of computing and comparing environmental damage, a moment of inspiration struck me. My old training in mathematics brought forth visions of logarithms, and with that, the conversation shifted to a far simpler potential design for measuring environmental damage and the flip side, positive impacts.

The result of this conversation and others is the proposed impact index that you will find outlined in this book. I've named the index in honor of Gifford, and in honor of the business school which he founded. In 2014 the school was renamed Pinchot University in honor of Gifford Pinchot I, creator of the U.S. National Forest Service, who, not coincidentally, is Gifford Pinchot III's grandfather.

Forward: The Happo-Dammo Ratio

by Gifford Pinchot III, founder of the Bainbridge Graduate Institute
bgi.pinchot.edu

Facing climate change we have three choices: Denial, Depression or Doing something about it. One of those is far more fun than the others.

We need an enormous amount of creativity to solve the problems of climate change. Because people are way more creative when they're having fun, the solution is this: lighten up, forgive whoever you're blaming for climate change, and do something about it. Just remember to have fun doing it.

For example, many years ago I was at a weeklong conference when my son called me up and said, "Dad you can't spend the entire weekend inside in weather like this; come out and play with me. I'll show you how my generation has fun."

He took me to a disk golf course. For those of you who don't know, disk golf is a game that's played just like regular golf but instead of hitting balls into a hole, you throw little frisbees into a basket.

We played 36 holes of disc golf that day, then we went down to the lake, took off our clothes, swam out to a little island, climbed up a cliff, and ran around on top of the cliff until the Yellow Jackets chased us away. We dove back into the water and swam back to our clothes.

As I was putting on my clothes **I had a revelation**. I told myself that we had had the same amount of fun as if we played traditional golf and taken a dip in the club pool, but the courses were very different. No bulldozers were used to make the course that we had played on. No sand was hauled from distant places. No pesticides, fungicides or herbicides were used to maintain it. There was no electricity, no concrete, no pumps, no golf carts or paved paths.

Indeed, the environmental damage in creating the disc golf course we played on that day was one thousand times less than the damage done in creating a normal golf course .

Sitting on the beach and putting on my clothes after swimming back from the island, a formula appeared in my mind, the **Happo Dammo Ratio**. It's the ratio of happiness created by any activity divided by the amount of damage done by that activity.

This turns out to be a very important ratio, because what we have to do for civilization to survive is to get much better at the Happo Dammo Ratio. If we can provide more human satisfaction with less damage to the environment we are well on the way to solving our environmental problems.

We only have to cut greenhouse gas emissions to $1/5^{th}$ of what they are today to solve the problem of climate change. Given the example of getting 1000 times better, I think a 5 to 1 overall reduction in emissions is doable. There is hope, if we focus on what really makes us happy.

What makes us happy? Sure we need food, warmth, water, air, health, and things like that, but we don't need a lot of those things before other factors become much more important to our happiness. Once our survival is taken care of, it's relationships, meaning, respect, and freedom that make us happy.

To give you an example of that, on average a person who is terminally ill is happier than a person who has divorced in the last two years. The quality of relationships is more important than whether we are rich or poor, or whether we are healthy or terminally ill. Isn't that an interesting commentary on what it means to be a human being! We are deeply social creatures.

Another example from years ago. When I was an adolescent I believed I needed a 400 horsepower car to pick up girls. Shows what I knew about women. ;-) But I think this error illustrates a more general point. In this society we are using things to get better relationships, when that's really both damaging and ineffective. Look at the ads. So many hint that buying this or that will make you popular, powerful or get you great sex. However, being emotionally aware and caring about others is not only a more environmentally benign strategy, it is also much more effective.

It's much easier to know what it takes for people to get along. It's much more important to know what makes others feel good. It's much more important to manage relationships and have friends than to have a lot of stuff.

And if that's true, we can get to a much higher Happo Dammo Ratio if we just focus on what really makes people happy. **In the process we will save civilization.**

Table of Contents

MEASURING, AGGREGATING & COMPARING IMPACT.....................**1**
  CHAPTER 1. What and Where is Impact?......................................3
  CHAPTER 2. Measuring Impact..6
  CHAPTER 3. Comparing Impact 19
  CHAPTER 4. Aggregating Impact..21
ORDERS OF MAGNITUDE **24**
  CHAPTER 5. Orders of Magnitude in Mathematics 26
  CHAPTER 6. Orders of Magnitude of Impact................................33
THE PINCHOT IMPACT INDEX **36**
  CHAPTER 7. A New Measure of Impact......................................38
  CHAPTER 8. Measuring Impact from 0 to 7 39
  CHAPTER 9. Negative Impacts 46
  CHAPTER 10. Limited Choices, Broad Ranges.............................49
  CHAPTER 11. Rules of Thumb for Valuing Impact 50
  CHAPTER 12. Measuring Achieved Impact 53
  CHAPTER 13. Comparing Achieved Impacts 57
  CHAPTER 14. Aggregating Achieved Impacts 58
  CHAPTER 15. Net Impact 61
  CHAPTER 16. Aggregating Aggregations.................................63
  CHAPTER 17. Indirect Impact 65
  CHAPTER 18. P^nROI...69
  CHAPTER 19. More P^2s, P^3s, and P^4s...............................72
  CHAPTER 20. Final Thoughts 74
APPENDIX **76**
  CHAPTER 21. Objections..78
  CHAPTER 22. Utopia & Symmetry 86
  CHAPTER 23. The Choice of P^n...88
  CHAPTER 24. We Still Need IRIS 91
  CHAPTER 25. We Still Need GIIRS & B Corporations 92
  CHAPTER 26. PwC's TIMM Language......................................94
  CHAPTER 27. Other Limited Scales..97
  CHAPTER 28. Example Ratings / Sample Portfolio 99
  CHAPTER 29. Log Log Scales 110
  CHAPTER 30. Feedback & Conversations 112

MEASURING, AGGREGATING & COMPARING IMPACT

The history through the state of the art

CHAPTER 1.
What and Where is Impact?

What is *impact*?

Gifford Pinchot III challenges businesses, investors, and individuals to maximize our net impact and minimize our negative impact. To do that, we need some common method of measuring and comparing impacts across different projects.

The first problem of measuring, comparing, and aggregating impact begins with the unfortunate fact that there is no agreed upon definition of *impact*.

Many organizations claim to have an impact on the world. And most of them do, if you use the dictionary definition (*"having an effect on someone or something[1]"*), which includes both positive and negative impacts. For philanthropists and *impact investors* who seek out *impactful* organizations, their use of the term *impact* focuses primarily on positive outcomes, but sometimes on reducing environmental and social damage.

Impact for those groups can be defined as maximizing the wellbeing for the largest number of people and creatures. Sometimes that is defined as actions which bring about the best outcome for the people and planet. Others describe impact from a humanistic point of view: maximizing freedom of choice while eliminating exploitation and avoiding harm to others.

The commonality of these definitions is the concept of *doing good*. Doing good, as opposed to *doing harm[2]*.

---

[1] Dictionary.com - dictionary.reference.com/browse/impact.

[2] Or sometimes, *doing less harm*, e.g. a Prius burns less fuel, but none the less burns fossil fuel.

Impactful Organizations

The stereotype of impactful organizations are the public charities and private foundations of the nonprofit sector.

The Nature Conservancy conserves the lands and waters on which all life depends. The Carnegie Corporation funded tens of thousands of libraries, creating the public library system we take for granted today. The Bill & Melinda Gates Foundation aims to eradicate malaria specifically and improve global health in general.

Nonprofits are not alone in having impact. All democratic and socialist governments include programs which aim to be impactful.

In the U.S., Social Security, Welfare, Food Stamps, Head Start, Medicare, the G.I. Bill, U.S.D.A. inspectors, and the Peace Corp all aim to improve the lives of individual Americans, strengthen society as a whole, and in the case of the Peace Corp, provide an impact beyond the borders of the country itself.

Local governments have impact as well, starting with the local police and fire departments, ambulances, parks departments, road departments, and public schools. These programs keep people safe, happy, improve access to the community, and educate the citizens to allow participation by all.

The newest realm of impact is the private sector, specifically for-profit companies which aim to do good while earning a profit. This sector includes mission-driven profitable companies like Patagonia as well as profit-driven companies with impactful missions like Whole Foods.

In addition, there is a movement for public companies to report on their *environmental, social, and corporate governance*, with some of those efforts having measurable impacts.

The key point is that impact is not limited to any one type of organization or one sector of the economy. Impact (doing good) can be accomplished by nonprofit, for-profit and government organizations, or for that matter by any informally unorganized individuals.

CHAPTER 2.

Measuring Impact

When you start an organization whose goals include impact, the question quickly arises as to how to measure that impact.

Unfortunately, there is no simple solution for measuring impact.

Dollars Don't Work

Nonprofits and government programs are often measured by their total budgets. For-profits are often measured by their revenues and/or profits. Dollars are the common measuring system of commerce, but unfortunately, impact does not arrive with a price tag or value in dollars.

Many people have tried to convert impact into dollars, but ultimately that conversion has problems. Finding a value for any given impact leads to confusion at best, or arguments at worst. For example:

You installed solar panels on the roof of your warehouse, eliminating 1,000 tons of CO_2 emissions. How do you value those tons of CO_2? Do you use the market value from the California carbon exchange, the value from the European exchange, the current value of the carbon tax from British Columbia, or the value of CO_2 externalities computed by the UN. These values range from \$2/ton to \$100/ton. Which is *correct* and why?

Your medical device company sold 10 artificial kidneys, saving ten lives. What are those lives worth in dollars? The insurance industry measure lives in dollars, basing the value on the potential lifetime earnings of the person. Do you agree that saving the life of an 80 year old is worth less than a 20 year old? Probably not. What if that 20 year old lives in a slum in Nairobi, with a lifetime earning potential less than the next year's Social Security check for an 80 year-old American? In terms of impact, a human life should always be worth the same, regardless of place of birth or current home address.

Your car sharing company deployed 500 cars across Seattle. You calculate that this deployment will allow 50 cars to avoid being built. What is the value of a car that was never-built? On the other hand, these shared cars are driven by the members, not by hired drivers. What is the negative impact if that car sharing service eliminates the need for 50 taxi drivers? How do you compute the value of a job in general, and a taxi driver specifically?

Your organization plants trees to prevent desertification. The trees have no value as lumber or firewood, as they are intended to stand in place for the next century or more, holding the soil in place, pulling moisture up from the ground, holding back the desert. What is the value of each tree?

The government agency you work for provided food for 100 children, saving them from malnutrition. Studies have shown that malnutrition leads to a lower salary in adulthood. What is the value in dollars today for potentially increasing the salary of those children a decade from now? Is that really the best way to measure malnutrition anyway?

If it was not obvious before these examples, the difficulty in measuring impact in dollars should now be far clearer. It is certainly possible to sit around a conference table and set values for each impact, but two groups sitting around two tables in two separate rooms will likely result in two vastly different results, as the calculations will include somewhat arbitrary assumptions.

Within a single organization, where all the assumptions can be agreed upon (or mandated from above), dollars may be workable, but across organizations, those assumptions vary far too much to make dollars a workable measure for impact.

The Triple Bottom Line

In 1997, in *Cannibals with Forks: the Triple Bottom Line of 21st Century Business*, John Elkington created the concept of the *triple bottom line*, adding environmental and social impact to the traditional single bottom line of profits. The triple bottom line is often described succinctly as measuring *people, planet, and profits*.

This measure was proposed for for-profit businesses. It never found much of a following in the nonprofit or government sectors, where organizations do not typically focus on the financial bottom line.

When I first started mentoring at the *Bainbridge Graduate Institute* in 2011, the triple bottom line was the key measure of impact, as those MBA students worked on business plans of for-profit companies. In the last few years, however, the popularity of the concept has waned, as organizations have struggled to compute the environmental and social bottom lines in any consistent manner. Furthermore, as the environmental and social bottom lines are not easily measured in dollars, nor often measured in compatible units, the result are three incompatible measures that are difficult or impossible to relate to each other.

Adding to all this trouble is the fact that most of the mission-driven companies I work with are aiming for a specific impact, which too often does not fit neatly into an environmental component and a social component. For example, which line includes improving customer health? Does a solar-powered cellphone charger count solely as environmental impact? What if it is used to run a cellphone charging business in a developing world, creating an income for the business and saving time and money for the customers? Similarly, how do you split the impact of organic farming, which is better for the environment, but also better for the farmers and the farm workers?

After struggling with the fixed framework of fiscal, environmental, and social bottom lines across dozens of business plans and companies, I and others have fallen back to a simpler measure consisting of two parts: fiscal bottom line plus impact.

That *double bottom line* structure is simpler, but the open problem remains of finding a good measurement structure for the impact.

SROI

Another measure of impact was created in 1997, the *social return on investment*, a.k.a. *SROI*. This measure was created by REDF, a grant-making nonprofit based in San Francisco.

SROI aims to measure the amount of impact per dollar. It has grown beyond philanthropy to be used by mission-driven for-profit companies as a means to entice impact investors, often presented next to or in lieu of the fiscal return on investment.

I first came across this measure at the University of Washington's *Global Social Entrepreneur Competition*, a business plan competition of impactful for-profit companies created by students from around the world. Each company was required to present their SROI as a measure of their impact.

The problems with this measure were obvious after just a few presentations, as the first business plan claimed a $5 SROI, i.e. $5 worth of social (or environmental) good per $1 of investment. The second business plan claimed a $10 SROI. The fifth presentation claimed an amazing $250 SROI.

The impact of these plans varied from offset CO_2 emissions to poverty elimination to lives saved. To compute the SROI, each converted their intended impacts into dollars. It was the assumptions within those conversions which led to the 50x difference in SROI, far more than any justifiable difference in the efficiency of each business plan.

In fact, there were enough business plans presented that multiple plans used CO_2 emissions as their intended measure of impact, and the SROIs across those plans differed by more than 10x.

SROI is a variant of impact measured in dollars, and as that underlying measure does not work, neither does SROI.

IRIS

In 2008, as an aid to standardize the measurement of impact for impact investors, the Rockefeller Foundation gathered together Acumen, B Lab, and others to create the *Global Impact Investors Network* (a.k.a. *GIIN*) and within that organization created the *Impact Reporting & Investment Standards* catalog, better know as *IRIS*.

IRIS is a collection of impact measurements collected from over 40 sectors. It is an attempt to create a universal collection of metrics which any organization can use for their own internal or external measure of impact.

IRIS does not attempt to create a single universal measure of impact. Nor are you expected to compare or aggregate multiple metrics. Each metric in the catalog stands alone, useful by itself as a key component of a project or organization. IRIS provides a way to define and standardize each metric and it provides an identifier for each metric, so that the same metric can be compared and aggregated across multiple projects or across organizations.

For example, below is a single IRIS metric, *Client Individual: Total*, IRIS ID#PD2541.

Note that this example is not a metric with a direct impact like saving lives or planting trees. It is a rather mundane measurement of the number of clients the organization reached in a given time period. IRIS aims to be comprehensive in regards to measurements.

Note too that IRIS does not expect organizations to use all the metrics within that catalog, but instead expects them to choose a 5-10 metrics.

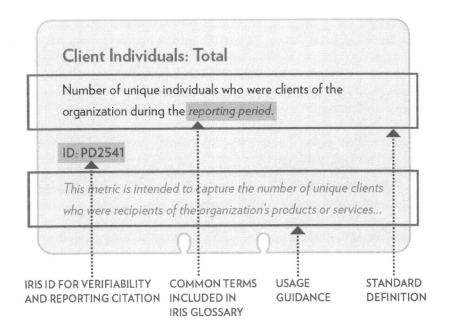

Client Individuals: Total

Number of unique individuals who were clients of the organization during the *reporting period.*

ID: PD2541

This metric is intended to capture the number of unique clients who were recipients of the organization's products or services...

IRIS ID FOR VERIFIABILITY
AND REPORTING CITATION

COMMON TERMS
INCLUDED IN
IRIS GLOSSARY

USAGE
GUIDANCE

STANDARD
DEFINITION

All of this standardization is helpful. It solves the problem of not having a standardized set of metrics to use within a single organization or consortium across organizations. However, as there are so many measures to pick from, and few which are comparable to each other, it does not solve the fundamental problems of measuring, comparing and aggregating impact between organizations.

The units on these metrics vary from people to hectares to tons, etc. IRIS makes no attempt to create a single universal measure across these metrics, nor does the standard include any suggestion on how to aggregate the values between metrics.

At best, by creating a standardized set of metrics for organizations to choose from, the hope is that organizations within the same sector will choose the same metrics, thus creating an apples to apples comparison. However, the IRIS 3.0 catalog contains 488 different metrics to choose from, and thus the odds of any two organizations choosing exactly the same set of 5-10 metrics is low.

GIIRS and B Corporations

The *Global Impact Investing Ratings System* (a.k.a. *GIIRS*) was created in 2010 to provide a *"comprehensive and transparent system for assessing the social and environmental impact of companies and funds"*.

The goal of GIIRS is to create a standardized measure of impact, as simple as a single number, which can then be used to compare impact between companies and investment funds, and to aggregate the total impact of a portfolio of companies.

Thousands of companies have GIIRS ratings, and dozens of funds are testing out the *B Analytics* system, which is a tool created to generate an aggregate GIIRS value across a fund's portfolio of investments. In addition, two dozen professional investment organizations are pioneering the use of the GIIRS rating as part of their investing screening process.

Underlying GIIRS is the same *B Impact Assessment* as used in the *B Corporation* certification process. Both GIIRS and B Corporation certification were created by and governed by B Lab, a nonprofit organization that serves *"a global movement of entrepreneurs using the power of business to solve social and environmental problems"*.

The B Impact Assessment is designed to measure for-profit companies. Specifically, it measures five areas of those organizations:

- Corporate governance
- Treatment of employees (a.k.a. "Workers")
- Interactions with the community
- Environmental impact
- Impact of the business model

The fifth of these measures is new to the 2014 version of the assessment, and not yet visible in every *B Impact Report*. Below is an example report, from Patagonia, a manufacturer of environmentally-conscious outdoor apparel, and also a pioneering *Certified B Corporation* and Delaware *Public Benefit Corporation.*

What makes us a better company?

B Impact Report

Certified since: December 2011

Summary:	Company Score	Median Score*
Governance	17	10
Workers	26	22
Community	31	32
Environment	35	9
Overall B Score	116	80

80 out of 200 is eligible for certification
*Of all businesses that have completed the B Impact Assessment
*Median scores will not add up to overall

The assessment awards points for actions and policies which are deemed by B Lab to have a positive impact in one of the five categories. Points are awarded, never subtracted. The questions on the assessment vary depending on some of the answers, including questions specific to manufacturing companies or service companies, and reallocating the points awarded for "Workers" depending on the size of the company. Thus in reality there is a matrix of assessments, which is tuned to the size and type of business being assessed. The goal of all that complexity is to create a single measure that allows one to compare different sized companies, from solo practitioners to medium size service-oriented companies, and even large public manufacturers.

The total possible points awarded is 200. A minimum of 80 points is required to be certified as a B Corporation. There is no minimum required to receive a GIIRS rating, which today uses exactly the same assessment as for B Corporations.

The benefit of the *B Impact Assessment* is the single rating, which can easily be compared and aggregated. In addition, the scoring system includes five subcomponents, which can be considered independently if that better matches an organization's mission.

However, all this standardization comes with the tradeoff that B Lab and its board of governors gets to choose the set of questions used to rate an organization, and the number of points each question is worth. This ultimately returns us to the question of comparing disparate impacts. For instance, which is more impactful: Sharing an ownership stake of the company with all the workers? Or performing an annual energy audit on your office? Is it better to give 15% of profits to charity, or to have a majority of your vendors be within 250 miles of your headquarters? Those are the types of answers in the assessment, and each has a number of points assigned from the potential 200 total points.

Mapping these answers to points is just as difficult and arbitrary as calculating impact in dollars, except for the constraint that there are only a maximum of 200 points allowed within the index, and the companies using the index have no control over how those points are allocated.

Ultimately, what works well for the B Impact Assessment is that it provides a list of impactful actions and policies for an organization, most of which the company has not yet adopted, which, if adopted, would create a more impactful organization. With those changes in place, any company with 80 or more points is measurably above average. The B Impact Assessment is thus a great tool for helping companies increase their impact or "doing good" in the world. However, the specific number of points above 80 is not a great measure of the total impact of the company, and as such, comparing ratings between companies and aggregating portfolios of companies all above 80 is today a near pointless exercise.

For example, is Patagonia a more impactful company at 116 points than The Honest Company at 92? Is Impact Hub Seattle with 100 points truly 7% more impactful than Impact Hub Boulder with 86 points (a difference of 14 points out of 200)? Does that make Impact Hub LA with 94 points 3% more impactful than Boulder? When used to compare organizations, points seem to be missing a factor of scale.

My own company, Fledge is a Certified B Corporation with a rating of 120. That is well above average, with a top 10% score for Community. Those scores are nice, but Patagonia and The Honest Company are far larger companies than Fledge, with over a million times more revenues, and with hundreds of thousands more customers. Where are those factors in the B Impact Assessment?

Outside of the Pinchot Impact Index presented in this book, the B Impact Assessment is the best universal measure we have, but far from a universal solution to actually *measuring* impact.

The Eye of the Beholder

Beauty, as they say, is in the eye of the beholder. In every day practice, impact is the same. For philanthropists and impact investors, the most common way to measure impact is "to know it when you see it".

When choosing amongst projects and organizations to support, philanthropists and impact investors make choices based on their own personal tastes. For example, a decision on Patagonia vs. The Honest Company depends far more on the investors' personal connection with the brands, their interest in apparel vs. organic baby supplies, their personal experiences hiking and changing diapers, and their own values on sustainability, allergies, and celebrity startups.

In practice, since there is no universal measurement system of impact, philanthropists and investors don't try to compare impacts, but rather **consider impact as a threshold** to be met in order for an organization to merit a grant or investment. An organization needs to be sufficiently impactful, as best as that measure can be described, then other factors are used to decide whether to provide the grant or make the investment.

Give Well[3], for example, helps philanthropists evaluate public charities. However, rather than measuring the impact of those charities, they leave that up to the donors, and instead focus on measuring internal efficiencies and operations.

This pattern is repeated in most of the impact investment groups where I participate, at Fledge in choosing its *fledglings*, and for my own personal impact investments. I see a deal, like its impact, and then move on to consider the quality of the team, the size of the opportunity, and the potential fiscal return on investment. I may then circle back to balance the amount and type of impact vs. the fiscal return, but once I have decided that the deal has sufficient potential impact, no further measuring of that impact is required.

As an impact investor and in my own philanthropy, I'd prefer impact to be a trusted, computed value, usable in all stages of the decision making process, rather than just a minimum threshold criterion.

Potential, Intended, and Achieved

Before leaving the discussion of measuring impact, I must point out that every organization has not just **one** issue of measuring impact, but **three issues**, as impact comes in three related levels.

First is the total **potential impact** given the product, service, or solution being implemented. For example, if my organization is solving the problem of access to healthy food (a.k.a. food deserts), then how many people in the whole country have this problem? E.g.,

---

[3] See givewell.org/criteria

My organization has the potential to improve the lives of 100,000 people. It is unlikely that my organization will solve this entire problem alone, but none the less it is useful for philanthropists and investors to understand the full scope of the problem and its flip side, the total potential impact.

Second is the **intended impact** of the organization. Is the intent to provide healthy food to a single neighborhood, a single city, single state, or the whole country? 10 million people might be hungry and potentially helped by the organization, but the organization might aim to help just 100,000 of them (because of budget restraints or other issues). If the problem is climate change, will the solution eliminate all anthropogenic carbon emissions, and methane emissions, and every other greenhouse chemical, or is the intent just to install a set of solar panels on the roof of one building?

Third is the **achieved impact**. What has truly been accomplished, and how much impact did that accomplishment actually do? Perhaps one solar panel replaced 1,000 KWh of electricity, which offset 10,000 tons of CO_2. 100,000 polypropylene hats from Patagonia came from recycling 10,000 soda bottles, thus saving two tons of trash from the landfill. 1,000 vaccines prevented 50 cases of malaria.

These three measures are often mixed together as we talk about measuring impact. SROI focuses on the intended impact. IRIS on the achieved impact. The *B Impact Assessment* on a mix of all three. No standard besides the Pinchot Impact Index proposes to measure, compare, and aggregate all three.

CHAPTER 3.

Comparing Impact

Once it is possible to measure impact, the inevitable next step is to start **comparing impacts**. These could be comparisons between projects within one organization, or comparing between whole organizations.

Metric by Metric Comparisons

Comparisons make the most sense when the metrics and underlying assumptions are identical between organizations.

For example, which is more impactful, Zipcar or Car2Go? Both are car sharing services, where the members drive the cars (unlike Uber or traditional taxis where the cars come with drivers). Zipcars are rented by the hour, picked up in parking spaces scattered throughout the city, and returned to the same parking space. Car2Gos are rented by the minute, parked on the street, and dropped off at any legal parking space in the same city.

Both services allow members to share cars, reducing the number of cars that must be manufactured. Both are helping increase the livability of cities and pushing up the density of those cities, both of which lead to lower per-capital consumption of energy. On the other hand, both are likely replacing trips that would otherwise be taken by bus, which has a negative impact on public transportation. And both use gas-burning cars that emit CO_2, another negative impact.

The customer experience of these two services are different, but in terms of operations, the businesses are nearly identical, and thus can be compared metric by metric, both fiscally and impactfully.

If only every comparison was this easy!

The Folly of Comparisons

Impact comparisons work when the metrics are identical, but quickly break down when metrics and impacts vary. For example, which of these is more impactful?

A. Saving 10 tons of CO_2
B. Volunteering for 10 hours

C. 10 subscribers to Zipcar or Car2Go
D. 1,000 fish farmed in a sustainable aquaculture

E. 10 human lives saved from Ebola
F. 10,000 trees saved from logging

How many trees equal one human life? How many volunteer hours equal one tree? How do you value fish vs. trees vs. health vs. cars?

These questions have obvious answers.

Comparisons Needed

Meanwhile, we do need a way to compare impacts. Every day, philanthropists and impact investors review potential grants and investments, and they want to make the most of their money, i.e. do the most good in the world.

These investors want a simple, single measure for doing good, like SROI or the B Impact Assessment. But they also want a measure that stands up to scrutiny, when in fact underneath that measure widely divergent goods are being funded, with one organization growing organic cranberries, another organization making clean burning cookstoves and a third bringing homes to communities after a storm. How can one truly compare the amount of good being done by each of these very different companies? The Pinchot Impact Index aims to fix this problem.

CHAPTER 4.

Aggregating Impact

Without a single value for measuring impact, it is also impossible to **aggregate the impact** across a portfolio of impact organizations, or similarly, a collections of impactful projects within a single organization.

The stakeholders of foundations, charities, and impact investment funds all expect reports on the success of their grants and investments. They want the single, simple measure of impact across the whole portfolio of investments, which is analogous to the fiscal return on investment.

They want an aggregate view of impact. They want the SROI-like value, summed and averaged across their portfolio.

But as we've seen when trying to measuring impact, no such simple value exists, and without it, aggregating impact is an unsolved problem.

Aggregation by Concatenation

If only philanthropists or impact investors limited themselves to a single investment or a single highly focused sector, then aggregating impact would be easy.

Just like in the question of comparing impacts, if all the key metrics are identical between two projects or two organizations, then aggregating impact is also simple. For example, if one solar power company offset 1,000 tons of CO_2 and one wind power company offset 2,000 tons of CO_2, then the total impact is an offset of 3,000 tons of CO_2.

However, the real world of philanthropy and impact investing is rarely this simple. Most foundations and funds invest in a far wider variety of impacts, and as such, face the unsolved issue of aggregating the total impact of their portfolios.

The typical solution today is aggregation by concatenation. If one organization in the portfolio saved 10,000 trees and another 1,000 lives, and a third 5,000 birds, then that total impact would be reported as saving 10,000 trees 1,000 lives, and 5,000 birds. Such a solution is accurate, but it does not feel much like a solution to the problem.

B Analytics

The GIIRS rating does have one method that a few dozen funds are testing, namely aggregating impact using the *B Analytics* tool. In this method, a portfolio receives a rating by taking the weighted average of the GIIRS ratings of each of its constituent investments.

For example, a portfolio containing equal parts Patagonia (116), The Honest Company (92), and Impact Hub Seattle (100) would have an aggregate rating of 103.

The *B Analytics* tool does compute weighted averages, which then take into account the size of each investment, and portfolio managers can change the weighting of the four sub-components within the GIIRS rating: Corporate governance, Workers, Community, Environment, and Business model.

Overall, the underlying concepts in this tool are exactly what every portfolio manager dreams of. However, the flaws of the GIIRS rating, as previous discussed, make the averages of those ratings far from a true aggregate rating, one which fails to solve the fundamental problem of aggregating 10,000 trees, 1,000 lives, and 5,000 fish.

ORDERS OF MAGNITUDE

Using mathematics to solve the measurement problem

CHAPTER 5.
Orders of Magnitude in Mathematics

It may seem a diversion to jump back to grammar school and relearn a bit of mathematics, but please bear with me for a chapter, as I propose that the answer to measuring, comparing, and aggregating impact lies in some simple mathematics.

1's, 10's and 100's

Back in grade school, you learned that numbers have "places". That the number 10 is really a 1 in the 10s column and a 0 in the 1s column. That 100 is a 1 in the 100s column, and zeros in the 10s and 1s columns. That 148 is one 100, four 10s, and eight 1s.

This place-value numbering system was an enormous breakthrough in mathematics when it was invented 5,000 years ago in Babylonia. Developed by Hindu and Arab mathematicians into the base 10 system we use today, it is now taught to young children and taken for granted by adults as "obvious".

Scientific Notation

Years later in junior high or high school, this concept of 10s reappeared in science class, under the name *scientific notation*. Remember 3×10^2 or 1.25×10^6?

Scientific notation is just an alternative way to write numbers, one far more convenient for very large and very small numbers.

Here's a reminder: $3 \times 10^2 = 300$.
Multiply 10 by itself twice ($10 \times 10 = 100$), and multiply that by 3.

$1.25 \times 10^6 = 1,250,000$.
Take a 1 followed by six zeros (1,000,000), which is the same as multiplying 10 by itself six times, and multiply that number by 1.25, remembering how to multiply with a decimal point.

Orders of Magnitude

What they may never have told you in school is that each time you multiply 10 by itself, you are increasing the value by an ***order of magnitude.***

The way we use that term is to say the difference between 10^4 and 10^5 is one order of magnitude. $10^4 = 10,000$. $10^5 = 100,000$. You multiply 10^4 by 10 to get 10^5.

How many orders of magnitude are there between 10^4 or 10^7? $10^4 = 10,000$. $10^7 = 10,000,000$. 10^7 is 1,000 times larger than 10^4. That is three orders of magnitude. 10 x 10 x 10, which equals 1,000. Note that you don't need to write out all the zeros to know the answer. You can simply subtract the exponents (7 – 4 = 3).

Once you learn to ignore the "10" and focus on the exponent, computing orders of magnitude is simple.

How many orders of magnitude are there between 10^9 or 10^{15}? Answer: 6. (15 – 9 = 6)

Naming Magnitudes

English has special names for some of the orders of magnitude.

- $10^2 = 100 =$ hundreds
- $10^3 = 1,000 =$ thousands
- $10^6 = 1,000,000 =$ millions
- $10^9 = 1,000,000,000 =$ billions (in American English)
- $10^{12} = 1,000,000,000,000 =$ trillions
- $10^{15} = 1,000,000,000,000,000 =$ quadrillions
- $10^{18} = 1,000,000,000,000,000,000 =$ quintillions
- $10^{21} = 1,000,000,000,000,000,000,000 =$ sextillions

In English, we put commas every three orders of magnitude when we write out the number in its long form, and except for one hundred, the named orders of magnitude also happen to be each separated by three orders of magnitude.

Comparing Magnitudes

If we want to compare numbers like 3×10^2 and 1.25×10^6 we can focus on the orders of magnitude and ignore the numbers before the 10^n (ignoring the 3 and the 1.25 in this example). In proper scientific notation, those values are always less than 10 and thus multiplying by that number does not change the order of magnitude.

So, what is the difference between 3×10^2 and 1.25×10^6? Four orders of magnitude, a.k.a. 10,000 (6-2 = 4 and 10^4 = 10,000). Ignoring the 3 and the 1.25, we can say that the second number is four orders of magnitude larger than the first number, which makes it about 10,000 times larger.

Let's try another example, this time leaving off any superfluous digits we will ignore. What it the difference between 10^9 or 10^{15}? We saw this question earlier. The answer is six orders of magnitude. Six orders of magnitude is a million. 10^{15} is thus a million times larger than 10^9. Or flipped around, there are a million billions in a quadrillion.

One more, to show this works for orders of magnitudes without names, the difference between 10^{11} and 10^4? Seven orders of magnitude (11 – 4 = 7), also known as ten million.

Visualizing Magnitudes

The numbers in the exponent act like the simple, linear measures we work with every day. However, do keep in mind that what they are actually measuring, the orders of magnitude, do not act like those typical measures.

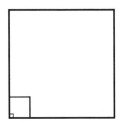

Each order of magnitude is 10 times larger than the one before it.

To help you visualize what this means, look at the diagram on the right. There are three boxes, each five times larger than the previous. I used just five times per box instead of 10 times, as otherwise the third box would not fit on the page. At this 5x scale, the fourth box would be about the height of the page, the fifth box the height of five pages, the sixth box taller than all the pages of the book laid end to end, and the seventh box so tall that it would take minutes to walk from one corner to another.

At 10 times scale per box, the lengths would not just double, but grow much much faster. We can again use the book itself to help visualize that scale. Keep the first box the same. The second box would then be twice as wide and twice as tall as the second box above (10x per side instead of 5x). The third box would then be about the width of the page. That would make the fourth box the width of 100 pages laid side by side, and just as tall. That is big enough to hold 67 printed books each with all their pages laid out side by side.

That may seem large, but keep going. The fifth box would be about a kilometer per side, the sixth ten kilometers per side, and the seventh box 100 kilometers per side. For comparison, a 100km by 100km square can hold both Rhode Island and Luxembourg with room to spare. A 100km by 100km box almost large enough to fit Belgium or Connecticut.

Seven steps from a small square to the size of a country. That is a fast growing scale!

Logarithms

One final tool from mathematics for our impact scale is the logarithm. A logarithm is a fancy name for the exponent in the order of magnitude.

Mathematicians would be precise and say the *base 10 logarithm*, as we are working with multiples of 10, but we can skip over those details.

Remember that 10^2 = 100, and 100 is just two 10s multiplied together. Logarithms focus on the number of times you multiply the ten. So, from the examples in the last section:

"log (10^2)" is simply 2 (which means multiple 10 **two** times)
log (10^6) = 6
log (10^{11}) = 11

Previously, when talking about orders of magnitude, we ignored the 3 in the value 3 x 10^2 and the 1.25 in the value 1.25 x 10^6. Logarithms let us keep that detail.

log (3×10^2) = 2.477
log (1.25×10^6) = 6.097

The results are not exactly 2 or exactly 6, because the factors of 3 and 1.25 were included in the calculation. Since those values are less than 10, their logarithms are less than 1, and simply get added to the value of the exponent.

So you multiply 10 more than two times, but less than three times, or more specifically:

$(3 \times 10^2) = (10^{0.477} \times 10^2)$

then,

log (3×10^2) = 0.477 + 2 = 2.477

You can check this by computing $10^{2.477}$ in a spreadsheet (type "10E2.477" into the spreadsheet) to see that the value is 300, which is what 3 x 10^2 means (3 x 100). (Note you might come up a little short, as I rounded the logarithm to 4 digits of precision.)

You need not fret over this level of detail, instead letting your calculator or spreadsheet worry about computing logarithms when they come up in future chapters.

And let's simplify this further, throwing away the overly mathematical and verbose notation of logarithms. Instead, let's simply talk about values L2, L6, and L11, or even better, write those values as L^2, L^6, and L^{11} to ensure we remember that they are orders of magnitude. Or $L^{2.477}$ or $L^{6.097}$ when we have fractional values.

In this form L^2 just means "one hundred" and we can think of $L^{2.477}$ as "somewhere in the hundreds". L^6 similarly means "one million" and $L^{6.097}$ means "a bit more than one million".

A Logarithmic Scale

We can now construct a ***logarithmic scale***. This is a scale where each value is not merely one time larger than the last value, but ten times larger.

Do note there is nothing magical or special about ten at the beginning the multiplier in the scale. With the mathematical tools we've talked about, we could just as easily create a scale where each value is 100 times larger than the last, or 1,000 times. Or we could (but we won't) create a scale that rises 33 times per value.

Before leaving this mathematical foray, let's take a look at a logarithmic scale that will be important later in the discussion: a scale that rises by a factor of 1,000. To distinguish it from the previous scale, let's call the levels T^0, T^1, T^2, ... T^n, where T reminds us of a *thousand*.

To minimize confusion, let's define two terms: **value** and **unit**. The *value* in the scale are the values T^0, T^1, T^2, ... T^n. Values can then be converted into *units*, such as:

T^0 = 1 unit *(the 0th power of any number equals 1)*
T^1 = 1,000 = 1 thousand units
T^2 = 1,000,000 = 1 million units
T^3 = 1,000,000,000 = 1 billion units
T^4 = 1,000,000,000,000 = 1 trillion units
T^5 = 1,000,000,000,000,000 = 1 quadrillion units
T^6 = 1,000,000,000,000,000,000 = 1 quintillion units
T^7 = 1,000,000,000,000,000,000,000 = 1 sextillion units

This scale grows quite quickly. And every value of the scale happens to correspond to a number of units with a name (in English), which will be convenient.

For now, we need not fret over what a unit represents, and instead end our lesson in logarithms and move back to measuring impact.

CHAPTER 6.
Orders of Magnitude of Impact

Impacts come in vastly different sizes. This is the key insight that allows us to create a usable impact index. Ending poverty, replacing fossil fuels in transportation, and achieving world peace are not just *slightly* larger than reusing shopping bags, carpooling, and volunteering at the food bank; they are *orders of magnitude* larger

If this isn't obvious, step back for a moment and think about two imaginary countries, each with 1 million citizens, where 50% of each country is considered to be poor. In country A, we eliminate poverty. No one is hungry, everyone has a home, everyone can afford to meet their basic needs. In country B, everyone is given a half dozen reusable, organic cotton shopping bags. Not everyone can afford to fill the bags with groceries, but plastic bags no longer litter their country.

We could use IRIS metric **PI4060** to measure both impacts. That metric is defined as the *Number of unique individuals who were clients of the organization during the reporting period.* In country A, we've directly impacted a half million citizens. In country B, all 1 million citizens (twice as many).

However that metric misses the scale of the impact. Not being poor is not just a little bit better than having a reusable shopping bag. It's not even just 10 times better. It is thousands or millions or billions times better.

Orders of magnitude better!

This is a bit of a contrived example, but showcases just how different two impacts can be.

Given such vast potential differences, let's look at what happens if we have an index that tells us what order of magnitude each impact falls into. For now, let's not fret over how those index values are chosen, (we will address this issue in the next section) and instead focus on how they might solve the problem of measuring and comparing impacts.

This example may at first seem a bit complex, but each step is simple.

First, suppose planting a hectare of trees has an index value of 3. Remember we are using a logarithmic scale, and to keep things simple, for this example the values rise by a factor of 10. $L^3 = 10^3 =$ 1,000 units.

Next, suppose sending a child to school has a value of 7. $L^7 = 10^7 =$ 10,000,000 units.

Lastly, suppose that we've used IRIS metric PI4127 to measure 3,200 hectares of trees and IRIS metric PI2389 to measure 525 children.

Combining the IRIS metrics and impact index, we can compute:

$$3,200 \text{ trees} = 3,200 \times 10^3 = 3.2 \times 10^6 \text{ units}$$
$$525 \text{ children} = 525 \times 10^7 = 5.25 \times 10^9 \text{ units}$$

What does this tell us? It says that the school impact was approximately 1,000 times larger than the tree impact (3 orders of magnitude is 1,000). I say *approximately* as I am ignoring the numbers 3.2 and 5.25 and focusing only on the order of magnitude. The difference between 5 and 3 is insignificant compared to the difference of 1 million (10^6) and 1 billion (10^9).

Let's look at a second example. Suppose solar-powered lanterns have an index of $L^2 = 10^2 =$ one hundred units. Supposed malaria vaccines have an index of $L^5 = 10^5 =$ one hundred thousand units. If we sell 70,000 lanterns and vaccinate 3,000 people, then we can say:

$$70,000 \text{ lanterns} = 70,000 \times 10^2 = 7 \times 10^6$$
$$3,000 \text{ vaccines} = 3,000 \times 10^5 = 3 \times 10^8$$

The difference in impact here is two orders of magnitude, which is approximately 100. *(Approximate, as we are again ignoring the 7 and the 3 and focuses solely on the orders of magnitude).* The vaccines are much more impactful than the lanterns, even though fewer vaccines are distributed than lanterns.

THE PINCHOT

IMPACT

INDEX

The proposed answer to
measuring, comparing, and aggregating impact
within and between organizations

CHAPTER 7.

A New Measure of Impact

We now have all the pieces needed to create a new measure of impact: logarithmic scales, a definition of impact (*doing good*), and an understanding of the problems involved in measuring, comparing, and aggregating impact

Since the idea for this new measure of impact was inspired by a conversation with Gifford Pinchot III during a extracurricular session at Pinchot University, I call this the **Pinchot Impact Index.**

Not surprisingly, this index is a logarithmic scale. Given the vast range of potential impacts in the world, from giving $1 to charity through to ending poverty, world peace, and more, this is an index which spans 42 orders of magnitude. To make that manageable, the index is a logarithmic scale, where each value is a factor of 1,000 units. As you will see, on this scale the important differences in impact become obvious.

The remainder of this book will provide the details of the index:

- How to assign a value for an impact
- How to use the index for measuring potential, intended, and achieved impacts
- How to compare those values
- How to aggregate impacts

Plus we will start the conversation on:

- What problems this index fails to solve
- What problems it creates
- What more is needed

CHAPTER 8.

Measuring Impact from 0 to 7

There are two innovations within the Pinchot Impact Index.

First, it is a logarithmic scale with a factor of 1,000 between each value. This coincides with the fundamental but often overlooked fact that different impacts differ in value not just by orders of magnitude, but by *multiple* orders of magnitude. That is, this index recognizes that impacts are not just different in scale, they are hugely, enormously different in scale.

Second, the scale extends only from 0 through 7:
P_0, P^1, P^2, P^3, P^4, P^5, P^6, and P^7.

Seven may sound like an odd choice, but it serves an important purpose. It condenses the number of possible measures, eliminating most of the potential arguments about which of two impacts is more important.

P_0 is no impact. It is the measure of inaction.

P^7 is nirvana, where everyone is as enlightened as Buddha, compassionate as Jesus, wise as Confucius, etc.

Given those two bookends, the scale is even smaller than it appears, with just P^1 though P^6 as available choices for all other impacts. From best downward, each level contains the following potential impacts:

P^7

This is a world where everyone is enlightened as Buddha, as compassionate as Jesus, as wise as Confucius, as smart as Aristotle. Or in other words, this is the ideal end state that every religion promises every believer. Heaven on Earth. Eternal bliss. Nirvana. Valhalla. Utopia.

P⁶

This is the near-utopian society dreamed of in many science fiction books (not including whatever calamity strikes). It is the worry-free days between episodes of Star Trek, where you can walk over to replicator and order any meal at any time, with no payment required. It is a world of abundance, money has no meaning. You want for nothing, and can spend your life pursuing self improvement and exploration. And people do so with great enthusiasm.

It is a world without disease, not even the common cold. A world without pollution. A world without further anthropogenic extinctions of wildlife. Where the deer and the antelope still play.

A world where people stop to watch the sunset, or a rainbow, or any of the other beautiful sights that nature provides.

Like Gifford mentioned in the forward, a world where relationships, meaning, respect, and freedom are what lead to happiness. In this world, everyone has a loving, caring community that they belong to.

Do note that like all of the levels in this scale, P⁶ represents not a single point on a graph, but a range of 1,000 units. Thus there are levels of utopia possible, all within P⁶, such as humanity in this state of bliss on Earth, or humanity spread across the galaxy. 7 billion people at peace in this state, or 7 million trillion in a Galactic Republic or Federation of Planets. Logarithmic scales have space for all these options without infringing on P⁷.

P⁵

Peace on Earth. No wars, no crime, no fear from others. Universal freedom of speech, press, and religion. Healthy lives, with vaccines and cures for all communicable diseases, and treatments or cures for all genetic disorders.

A world of balanced lives, where anyone who is capable of working has some meaningful to work to do. People have time for both work and relaxation. The world has no slavery, no indentured servitude, no sweatshops, no forced labor of any kind.

The world in Martin Luther King, Jr.'s dream, where people are judged by what they do and how they act, not what they look like, who their ancestors were, how they choose to live and pray, nor any other category of "us" and "them" we've yet to create.

A society where people act graciously and kindly toward each other. People engage in meaningful projects of worth. Art, science, and learning are abundant.

A sustainable civilization, where all resources are recyclable, leaving the planet as good or better for all generations.

P^5 is a far better world than we have today, but one that is still 1,000 times less perfect than the least utopian utopia.

This is a world where there is still scarcity, with some people having more than others, but no violent conflict to settle those disputes. A world where everyone can't have everything they want, whenever they want, but where all their basic human needs are met.

This is a far far better world than we live in today, but one that is reasonable to dream about achieving within the 21st Century. Such a goal is audacious, but not impossible.

Given P^6 seems unfathomably far from reality and P^7 an unreachable ideal, the Pinchot scale for all practical purposes is a 0-5 scale rather than 0-7. None the less, despite that limitation, P^5 is by definition 1 quadrillion (10^{15}) times better than the P_0 neutral status quo. That gives us a million billion units of measure, the use of which will be explained later.

P^4

A world without poverty. Everyone has their basic needs met of food, shelter, water, employment. A carbon neutral civilization, creating all its energy from renewable means.

In this world poverty is gone, but far from forgotten. There continues to be haves and have not, but with the difference that the needs of the nots are taken care of in some means.

Every child goes to school, every child has access to books, and access to at least some small bit of nature. All children have a childhood, no child is forced to work to feed his or her family.

This world continues to have violent conflicts, but limited to small groups, regionally. The fear of nuclear war is history. Borders change via the ballot box, not by tank and bomb.

Nearly all resources are managed sustainably. Plastics are truly recyclable. Textiles too. We no longer project an end to access to potassium, lithium, or other important resources.

The world is no longer losing forests, and ideally regaining forestland long ago cut down. The percentage of land used for farming is no greater than today. The amount of wildlife is increasing. Fish are a abundant, rather than on growing list of endangered species.

This is a less ambitious level of impact than P^5, but still quite a ways away from today's world. On the Pinchot scale, P^4 is 1,000 times less impact than P^5, but still 1 trillion times more than P_0.

P^3

This world has yet to solve the problem of poverty, but has found a way to feed everyone on Earth. Life overall is better, as polio, malaria, and other major diseases have been eradicated from the planet, like smallpox was in the 20th Century. There is even a pill that saves most people from the flu, the common cold, and other routine viruses.

A world where renewable energy has become the norm, with the legacy carbon fuels on the decline. Similarly, air and water are trending cleaner. Topsoil is no longer an endangered resource. Farming is a perpetually sustainable system.

A world where every world citizen has a voice in their community, a right to select their own leader, and collectively a right to change the borders of their country, with a ballot, not a gun.

Compared to the 20th Century, the differences in the P^3 world are as vast as the differences between the 19th and 20th Century.

Lifespans are longer and healthier. Researchers figured out why some people live 100 years, and packaged up in the answer in a pill. If your kidneys, heart, liver or lungs give out before then, grow a replacement in a vat from your own stem cells.

Technology is even more ubiquitous and helpful. You can have a human-like conversation with Siri on your iPhone 99S, or your iRetina 2 or other implantable connection to the Net.

The world continues to get smaller, with supersonic transportation, self-driving cars, and finally, flying cars, promised back in the 1962 World's Fair.

The world will get flatter too, as the middle class grows by billions, expanding global production, but more and more adopting sustainable methods and automation, as the legions of poor workers in sweatshop-like conditions have nearly all been pulled out of poverty.

As we drop down to P^3, the plausibility rises, but remains a dreams that will take quite an effort to achieve. On the Pinchot scale, P^3 is just 1 billion units away from P_0.

P^2

A world that addresses the major system issues not already mentioned. No homelessness. No unemployment. No tyranny. Universal access to healthcare. Vaccines for all major diseases.

A world of healthy communities, where members support one another, whether it be family, friends, religious groups, etc.

Violent crime is newsworthy in its rarity, including domestic violence and other hidden abuses.

No digital divide. Transparent governments. Transparent industry.

Sustainability in all supply chains is considered an important factor. Reporting of corporate governance issues, a norm. Impact investing is just called investing.

The impacts of P^2 are 1 million times larger than P_0, doing nothing. Many of these are the *big hairy audacious goals* (BHAG) we see charities, governments, and beneficial corporations promise to meet. Note that despite many such promises, few of those goals have ever been met in full.

P^1

P^1 encompasses every other impact that is better than doing nothing, but which is not worthy of being categorized as a P^2, P^3, P^4, P^5, P^6, or P^7.

If the impact is measurably positive, but is not fixing a systemic flaw or systemic injustice, or it is not completely changing the world, then it is valued a P^1.

Remember, on the Pinchot scale P^1 encompasses 1,000 units, i.e. three orders of magnitude of impact. What that means is that if an impact is tiny, worth just 1 unit, then it falls into P^1. 5 units, and it still falls into P^1. On hundred times better yet, 500 units, still P^1. Until an impact merits at least 1,000 units on this scale, it gets compacted down to a value of P^1.

Nearly all of what nonprofit, government, and mission-driven for-profit organizations do today falls into category P^1. They are nice, and good, and worthy of our respect. They help people trying to survive in the moment. But they are not large enough upon themselves to fundamentally change the world.

P_0

The world we hope to live in next year, when the damage of today's world is no longer a daily occurrence.

Additionally, P_0 is this is the measure of inaction, as in no action or net zero impact.

CHAPTER 9.
Negative Impacts

In CHAPTER 1, we defined impact as doing good, and thus always positive. Meanwhile, the world is full of problems, full of unsustainable practices, full of negative impacts.

We can use the same logarithmic scale to capture this damage, using negative numbers from -1 through -7. To ensure we do not mistake these for the positive impacts, I call these $_{-1}P$, $_{-2}P$, $_{-3}P$, $_{-4}P$, $_{-5}P$, $_{-6}P$, and $_{-7}P$, with the negative number as a subscript prefix. This mirrors the general rule in the design of graphs, where down and to the left is considered bad, up and to the right is good.

$_{-1}P$

The value $_{-1}P$ mirrors P^1, encompasses any negative impact that is not so damaging as to merit being categorized as $_{-2}P$, $_{-3}P$, $_{-4}P$, $_{-5}P$, $_{-6}P$, or $_{-7}P$.

These are the everyday impacts of: driving to work in a fossil-fueled car (yes, even a Prius, or a coal-powered Tesla). Buying non-organic produce. One suburban lawn. Not recycling. Paving a parking lot. Using disposable diapers. Plastics.

$_{-2}P$

One thousand times more damage than $_{-1}P$, and three orders of magnitude in scale. This encompasses systemic damage. Industrial agriculture as a whole, factory farming, the oil and gas industries, coal, sweatshops, slavery.

Discrimination, social injustice, sex trafficking, organized crime, racketeering, Enron, and the broken systems which created the financial meltdowns of 2007, 1929, and multiple Panics of the 19th Century.

-3P

Plague, global famine, major regional war, minor nuclear war.

Any "black swan" disruption of 100 million lives or more, such as a city-sized asteroid strike, pandemic, or tsunami striking New York City or London or Shanghai.

The extinction of honey bees. Any depletion of an important natural resource, e.g. no more oil, no more copper, no more uranium, the last bag of potassium, etc.

Climate change which costs more than 10% of global GDP to deal with.

-4P

World War III.

Collapse of the global economic system. All banks collapse. All records of bank balances, stock ownership, bonds, real estate, etc. are wiped away.

A solar flare wipes out the electrical grid on half the planet. The Internet ceases to exist.

The ocean's ability to sustain life is severely limited. The rain forests dry up. Deserts cover half the Earth.

1 billion people die within one day, week or year.

Return to totalitarian rule as the majority form of government.

-5P

More than 1 billion lives are lost. Global pandemic. Global thermonuclear war. Major asteroid strike. Runaway greenhouse effect or the next ice age begins.

The end of modern civilization.

-6P

Beyond the end of modern civilization, the end of all civilizations.

The extinction of all human life.

The extinction of every other sentient species... everywhere.

-7P

The extinction of all life on earth.

The end of the universe.

Or anything worse.

CHAPTER 10.

Limited Choices, Broad Ranges

The range of $._7P$ through P^7 spans from the end of all life through enlightenment. It is thus vast, while at the same time limited to just fifteen values.

That limitation is important. It forces us to think about the value of an impact at an exceedingly high level, rather than arguing whether my global health project is slightly more or less impactful than your solar power project. If I like global health and you like cleantech, does it really matter whether my project scores 10% higher or lower on SROI or via some IRIS measure or whether my company's GIIRS rating is 10 points higher than yours?

With just five choices for positive impacts (P^6 and P^7 being out of reach), it is highly likely our two projects have identical index values. That is helpful. It lets us then focus on how much of our impact is achieved vs. intended. **Achieving impact is far more important than arguing about whose impact is more important**.

1,000 units per value

In the Pinchot Impact Index, each value spans 1,000 underlying units. Units are not people or dollars or trees or fish or any other concrete item. They are just units, useful to help us grasp what it means that a P^3 is 1,000 times more impactful than a P^2, or 1 million times more impactful than a P^1.

Units are there to remind us that impacts span orders of magnitude.

The index was specifically chosen to put three orders of magnitude within each value to make those orders of magnitude far clearer. It also helps simplify the math when the time comes later to aggregate impacts together, and to measure whether intended impacts are being achieved.

CHAPTER 11.
Rules of Thumb for Valuing Impact

What value should you assign to your impact?

There are too many problems in the world. There are also too many proposed solutions for us to create a complete list of impacts and their corresponding values. Instead, we define each benchmark and leave the assignment of values up to you.

Here are a few rules of thumb to help you decide:

RULE 1- The values you assign to impacts are always whole numbers. Your only choices are P_0, P^1, P^2, P^3, P^4, P^5, P^6, and P^7. (Or the negative values if you are calculating damage.)

RULE 2- The most likely answer is P^1. Remember, P^1 spans every impact from small (1 unit) to 999 times larger, three orders of magnitude.

RULE 3- If your solution helps individual people or small groups of people, it is likely a P^1. A P^2 must not only create systemic change, but impact everyone interacting within that system.

RULE 4- Remember, a cure for the flu is only a P^3. Same for the electrification of the developed world, i.e. the inventions and commercialization of the light bulb, electric generator, electric grid, and electrical outlet. P^3 is a world-changing level of impact.

RULE 5- To be a P^4, it is not good enough to solve poverty in a single country. You have to at least intend a solution for the whole world.

RULE 6- I wish you were working on a P^5, but neither the United Nations nor the World Bank have come close to creating world peace. A few of their initiatives may intend to be as large as a P^4, but despite the massive resources of those kinds of organizations, few have the funding and ability to be larger than a P^3.

RULE 7- Remember that the world spans over 7 billion people living in more than 200 countries. Solving a problem completely in one country is orders of magnitude simpler than solving it worldwide. For a global impact, I'd argue the difference is at least three orders of magnitude, dropping any P^2 for a single country (or region) down a whole index value to a P^1, any similarly, dropping a P^3 down to a P^2.

RULE 8- When it comes to assigning values to your existing projects, **don't be greedy**. Better to do some good in the world with a P^1 or a few P^1s than to sit around and argue that your impact deserved a P^2. Leave it to the history books to decide the actual measure of impact.

RULE 9- When it comes to creating a new project or expanding your project **be greedy and bold**. Aim high! If you can see how to scale your impact up dramatically and to radically change lives by improving the system, go for it. Remember, a P^2 is 1,000 more impactful than a P^1. A P^3 is 1 million times larger. Achieving 10% of a P^3 is equal to completing 1,000 P^1s.

Potential, Intended, and Achieved

Back in CHAPTER 2, a distinction was raised about three measures of impact within a single organization. The three levels were defined as:

- **Potential** impact – The level of impact if the problem were to be solved everywhere it exists.
- **Intended** impact – The level of impact your organization plans to achieve in the world, when it has succeeded.
- **Achieved** impact – The level of impact achieved to-date.

When assigning values for your organization's impacts, make clear distinctions between the potential, intended, and achieved impacts. For each impact, you should have three separate values.

CHAPTER 12 explains how to take an intended impact and create a value for an achieved impact. Thus you just need to pick two values for each impact: potential and intended.

Do those impacts lie within the same order of magnitude? Within two orders of magnitude? If so, then assign them the same value. If not, then the intended impact will be one or more values smaller.

For example, the problem you are trying to solve could be global, but your plans are limited to one country or one city. Solving a problem globally is many orders of magnitude more complicated than targeting a solution in a single country or region (see RULE 7). A solution in America may not even work in China or India or Africa.

Moving from the hypothetical to a specific example, over 1 billion households cook their meals using three stones and an open fire. Your organization intends to sell clean burning cookstoves throughout Africa. That impact, when achieved, would span hundreds of millions of households and over 1 billion people. However, despite creating a distribution network across dozens of countries in Africa, that would still leave hundreds of millions of homes untouched in the Americas and Asia, lands with vastly different types of cuisine (tortillas, nan, and stir fry) and massive differences in cultures.

Replacing three stone cooking globally with clean burning cookstoves is a P^3 impact. That is the **potential** impact. An organization **intending** to do this for all of Africa would have an intended impact of P^2. (Africa is big, but there are similar needs elsewhere in the world, see RULE 7) A smaller organization targeting a single country would have an **intended** impact of P^1. (Repeat RULE 7 again, as a single country is far smaller than a whole continent.)

CHAPTER 12.

Measuring Achieved Impact

Between the description of the values in CHAPTER 8 and the rules in CHAPTER 11, you should have some idea what value to assign to your organization's intended impact.

That is a good number to tout, but it doesn't answer the question of how big an impact has been actually achieved.

Values and Units

To measure achieved impact, we will convert the index value to the corresponding number of units, then multiply by a percentage. For the calculations, a P^1 equals 1,000 units, a P^2 equals 1,000,000 units, a P^3 is 1 billion units, and so on increasing by a factor of 1,000 per level.

Similarly and symmetrically, a $_{-1}P$ equals -1,000 units, $_{-2}P$ equals negative 1,000,000 units, $_{-3}P$ negative 1 billion units, etc. downward by 1,000 per level.

For completeness, note that a value of P_0 contains 0 units. (Further note that P_0 does not span even a single order of magnitude. $P_0 = 0$ units = no impact. This is different from the other values for P, each of which contains three orders of magnitude of values.)

A P^n is a P^n

Every P^1 equals 1,000 units. Every P^2 equals 1,000,000 units. Etc. Each of these values spans three orders of magnitude of impact, but no consideration is given to whether an impact is at the small end or large end of those magnitudes.

This is on purpose. It avoids the arguments around whether one solar panel on one roof is better or worse than one clean burning cookstove or one vaccine.

Each is a P^1. The same P^1. The same 1,000 units. As is 10 solar powered homes, 100 clean cookstoves, and 500 vaccines.

0.01%, 1%, 10%, 50%, 100%

However, we are going to include a factor for how much of an intended impact is actually achieved. To do this, we use a discrete, limited set of choices in order to avoid arguments over subjective opinions.

To measure actual, achieved impact, pick the largest of the following:

- If you have **achieved any meaningful impact**, then measure the impact as **0.01%** of the units of the intended impact.
  0.01% is 1/10,000th of the index value in units
- If you have achieved **more than 1%** of the total intended impact, then measure **1%** of the units
  1% is 1/100th of the index value in units
- If you have achieved **more than 10%** of the total intended impact, then measure **10%** of the units
  10% is 1/10th of the index value in units
- If you have achieved **more than 50%** of the total intended impact, then measure **50%** of the units
  50% is half of the index value in units
- If you have achieved **everything you've intended to** then measure **the full 100%** of the units

These are the only values you are allowed to use. For measuring impact, you **can not** claim your project is 25% complete, or 33%, or 49% or 99%, or any other value other than 0.01%, 1%, 10%, 50%, or 100%.

A P^2 equals 1,000,000 units and thus these measures are:

- 0.01% of P^2 = 100 units
- 1% of P^2 = 10,000 units
- 10% of P^2 = 100,000 units
- 50% of P^2 = 500,000 units
- 100% of P^2 = 1,000,000 units

A P^1 equals 1,000 units and thus these measures are 1,000 times smaller:

- 0.01% of P^1 = 0.1 units
- 1% of P^1 = 10 units
- 10% of P^1 = 100 units
- 50% of P^1 = 500 units
- 100% of P^1 = 1,000 units

To compute the values for a P^3, you can simply multiply the values of a P^2 by 1,000, and repeat that again by a factor of 1,000 for a P^4 and yet again for a P^5.

The values for the negative impacts are perfectly symmetric with the positive impacts, only negative instead of positive.

Remember the 80/20 Rule

When choosing the percentage completion of a project, remember that most of the time the first 80% of the results require only about 20% of the effort. Achieving 95% of the results typically requires a bit less than 50% of the effort. Unless some virtuous cycle exists to help, the last 5% is tough.

For example, despite the benefits of the telephone, it took over 100 years before the telephone achieved a 90% adoption rate in the United States, and landline telephones never reached every U.S. home. Neither did televisions. Nor the electricity grid.

From the world of global health is the story of polio. Smallpox was declared eradicated in 1980, after 250 years of effort. After that success, in 1988 the quest turned toward polio. Twenty-six years later, in 2014, there were still 325 cases of polio reported worldwide, across eight countries. We can likely expect ten more years before we see the last case of polio.

That last 5%, 2%, and 1% can truly be as much effort as all the work before then.

1% of P^n is larger than a whole P^{n-1}

To repeat and augment RULE 8 from CHAPTER 11, don't be greedy when assigning values or percentages to your existing projects . Each index value is 1,000 times greater than the last. Thus completing even 1% of a P^2 impact is greater than completing a P^1 impact. Ten times greater.

That may sound odd at first, but we did say that each level is 1,000 times larger than the previous, and 1% of 1,000 times is 10 times.

That factor of 1,000 is why the odd-looking 0.01% was included in the list of choices, as 0.01% of P^n is 10% of the P^{n-1}. For sample, P^2 impact that has made 0.01% progress is equal to 10% progress of a P^1 impact. 0.01% x 1,000,000 units = 100 units

CHAPTER 13.
Comparing Achieved Impacts

Comparing potential impacts is simple, since there are just fifteen potential values, $_{-7}P$, $_{-6}P$, $_{-5}P$, $_{-4}P$, $_{-3}P$, $_{-2}P$, $_{-1}P$, P_0, P^1, P^2, P^3, P^4, P^5, P^6, P^7. All potential impacts are one of these values.

Comparing intended impacts is just as simple, as they too are one of the fifteen possible values.

Given the *0.01%, 1%, 10%, 50%, 100%* rule, comparing two achieved impact is nearly as trivial. Simply convert the two impacts into units, compute the percentages, and compare the resulting number of units.

You might think that under this system a lot of organizations will end up with the same impact score. Yes, they will. That is by design.

The goal of the Pinchot Impact Index is to create a course grained measure that can be used to showcase the goodness across any type of impact.

Tie scores (as long as they are positive values) are a good way for everyone to recognize that important progress is being made.

All positive progress is good.

The world is far better off if we spend our time making positive impacts in the world, rather than arguing over whether my organization's impact is slightly larger or slightly smaller than yours.

CHAPTER 14.
Aggregating Achieved Impacts

Aggregating multiple impacts is not quite as simple as making comparisons, but can be easily done with a scientific calculator or spreadsheet.

The same calculation works for potential, intended, and achieved impacts:

1. Calculate the number of units in each impact
2. Calculate the sum of all these units
3. Calculate the logarithm (in base 10) of the sum
   We use base 10, even though the Index is base 1,000, because calculators may have a $\log_{10}$ button, but never a $\log_{1,000}$ button, and most spreadsheets have a LOG10 function, but no LOG1000 function.
4. Divide the logarithm by 3
   Why 3? Because it divides the exponent by 3, which is the equivalent of dividing the number by $10^3 = 1,000$. That converts $\log_{10}$ to $\log_{1,000}$.
5. Write out the answer as P^n

For example, the aggregate of impacts of **five P^1s**:

$P^1 + P^1 + P^1 + P^1 + P^1$
1. Each $P^1 = 1,000$ units
2. $1,000 + 1,000 + 1,000 + 1,000 + 1,000 = 5,000$ units
3. $\text{Log}(5,000) = 3.699$
   Why? $\text{Log}(5 \times 1,000) = \text{Log}(5) + \text{Log}(1,000) = 0.699 + 3 = 3.699$
4. $3.699 \div 3 = 1.23$
5. $P^1 + P^1 + P^1 + P^1 + P^1 = P^{1.23}$

This calculation is where the logarithmic scale finally becomes evident. This is because to aggregate the values, you can't simply add the exponents ($P^1 + P^1 + P^1 + P^1 + P^1$ is not equal to P^5), nor take an average ($P^1 + P^1 + P^1 + P^1 + P^1$ is not the average of 1, 1, 1, 1, and $1 = P^1$). To compute the true sum, you have to do the unit conversion and logarithm.

Remember, **it takes one thousand P¹s to equal a single P².**

1. Each P^1 = 1,000 units
2. One thousand P^1s = 1,000,000 units
3. Log (1,000,000) = 6
   Remember, 1,000,000 = 10^6 and Log (10^6) = 6
4. 6 ÷ 3 = 2
5. 1,000 P^1s = P^2

Going back to the first example, let's aggregate (add) the **five P¹s with a single P²:**

$$P^1 + P^1 + P^1 + P^1 + P^1 + P^2$$
1. Each P^1 = 1,000 units, P^2 = 1,000,000 units
2. $P^1 + P^1 + P^1 + P^1 + P^1 + P^2$ = 1,005,000 units
3. Log (1,005,000) = 6.002
4. 6.002 ÷ 3 = 2.0001
5. $P^1 + P^1 + P^1 + P^1 + P^1 + P^2 = P^2$

The sum is basically P^2. We could be specific and report this sum as $P^{2.0001}$, but .0001 is too tiny to fret over. Remember, when it comes to values, don't be greedy. Instead, remember again that a P^2 is so much bigger than a P^1, that five P^1s are trivial in comparison to that single P^2.

Let's try another example, this time for some partially complete, achieved impacts. **10% of a P¹, 50% of a P¹, plus 0.01% of a P².**

1. 10% of a P^1 = 10 units.
   50% of a P^1 = 500 units.
   0.01% of a P^2 = 100 units.
2. Sum = 610 units
3. Log (610) = 2.78
4. 3.699 ÷ 3 = 0.93
5. Aggregate = $P^{0.93}$

This result demonstrates that this index is not really limited to just fifteen values, but can take on fractional values as well. What can we say about a $P^{0.93}$? Quite a lot. We know it not quite as large as a P^1, and by now we should have some intuition on how big an impact a fully-implemented P^1 truly can be, and how even a fraction of a P^2 is still very impactful.

We also know this value is much closer to a P^1 than a P^0. Don't let the leading 0 in 0.93 fool you. This isn't no impact, it's quite a lot.

One last example. Imagine it is a few months later when both **P^1 projects are at 50%, and that P^2 project has now completed more than 1%:**

1. 50% of a P^1 = 500 units.
   1% of a P^2 = 10,000 units.
2. Sum = 10,500 units
3. Log (10,500) = 4.02
4. 4.02 ÷ 3 = 1.34
5. Aggregate = $P^{1.34}$

The aggregate is now above a single fully-completed P^1, and higher than the $P^{1.23}$ from the aggregate of five completed P^1s in the first example.

Personally, this is the where I find this index to be most useful. We finally have a way to aggregate the impact across multiple projects and multiple organizations. An aggregation that sums into a single, easily understood value. And a value that can be compared within and between organizations.

CHAPTER 15.

Net Impact

The examples in the last chapter aggregated only positive impacts. Unfortunately, much of the impact in the world continues to be focused on solutions that are "less bad" than the status quo.

Driving a Prius is not a positive impact; it's a smaller negative impact. So is driving an all-electric Leaf or Tesla, if any of your electricity is generated from non-renewable sources.

The same is true for switching to LED light bulbs, or turning down the thermostat in the winter, or any other energy conversation project which lessens the negative impact of burning oil or gas or coal.

Even when we look at projects like organic farming, we still need to account for the shipment of the goods to market. Unless that is done by solar-powered trucks, there is likely a negative impact to be accounted for.

The net impact of a project can be computed by aggregating both the positive and negative impacts within the project. The steps to do this are only slightly different from the previous chapter:

1. Calculate the number of units in each impact,
   positive or negative, using the 0.01%, 1%, 10%, 50%, 100% rule
2. Calculate the sum of all these units
3. Calculate the logarithm (in base 10) of the sum,
   or $-\log(-\text{sum})$ if the sum is negative,
   as logarithms of negative numbers are not defined
4. Divide the logarithm by 3
5. Write out the answer as $_{-n}P$ or P^n

For example, let us calculate the **net impact** of a project with **50% of a P^1 complete, plus three components that are each 10% of a $_{-1}P$.**

1. 50% of a P^1, = 500 units.
   10% of a $_{-1}P$ = -10 units. Three of these = -30 units.
2. Sum = 470
3. Log (470) = 2.67
4. 2.67 ÷ 3 = 0.891
5. Aggregate = $P^{0.891}$

The difference here is small compared to the $P^{0.899}$ for a half completed P^1. Change the balance of positive and negative impact completion, and the story is different. I.e. **aggregate a 10% complete P^1s and three 50% of a $_{-1}P$.**

1. 10% of a P^1, = 10 units.
   50% of a $_{-1}P$ = -500 units. Three of these = -1,500 units.
2. Sum = -1,490
3. -Log (1,490) = -3.17 [careful with the negative signs!]
4. -3.17 ÷ 3 = -1.06
5. Aggregate = $_{-1.06}P$

The result is slightly worse than one whole $_{-1}P$.

This is exciting! We now we have a tool for aggregating both positive and negative impacts within a single project, or across a whole organization, or even within an entire sector. The aggregation is boiled down to a single value which we can easily compare with other impacts.

CHAPTER 16.
Aggregating Aggregations

When aggregating impacts, the Pinchot Impact Index allows you to sum up as many disparate projects as you have to measure. This could lead to some organizations gaming the system, aggregating hundreds of thousands of individual projects to compute their total impact. We need some rules of thumb to prevent such impact-washing.

For example, there are over 1,000 employees at the Bill & Melinda Gates Foundations. It is possible to value the impact of each of those employees. If each had an intended impact of a P^1, the aggregate value be P^2, as by definition 1,000 P^1s equals a P^2.

Similarly, an organization with 100 active projects may choose to divide each of those projects into 10 measurable pieces. That would then create 1,000 measurements, which when aggregated would again have this over-aggregation issue.

To eliminate this issue, the rules for aggregating across projects are as follows:

AGGREGATION RULE A- When aggregating **within a single project**, divide that project into as many subcomponents as you'd like. Using the measuring and aggregation rules as described to assign as accurate a value as possible for the whole project.

AGGREGATION RULE B- When aggregating **between projects**, each project must be assigned a whole, round number (see RULE 1) for potential and intended impact; and for achieved impact, a percentage estimating the progress project as a whole, following the rules described in CHAPTER 12.

AGGREGATION RULE C- For large, complex organizations with multiple divisions, consider replicating these rules across entire divisions, assigning a single value per division rather than aggregating the values for all the projects within that division. The aggregate impact measure for the whole organization should follow the **existing hierarchy** within the organization.

The goal here is to accurately report on the true impact of any single organization. Use reasonable judgment to decide which projects deserve to be aggregated together. And in aggregations, continue to follow RULE 8, limiting the greediness of the final aggregate value.

CHAPTER 17.
Indirect Impact

Not all organizations' efforts have a direct impact. Some organizations are suppliers or vendors or service providers to other organizations who do have a direct impact.

Two simple examples of this are **Fledge**, the business accelerator which I created and manage, and **Impact Hub Seattle**, the co-working space where Fledge and other impactful organizations operate.

Fledge provides money, guidance, and support to impactful startup. Fledge does not directly save lives, clean the environment, or improve anyone's health. Our impact is all indirect, through the work of the "fledglings", or in some cases, indirectly one step further removed, as some of those companies are service providers to the organizations that have the input.

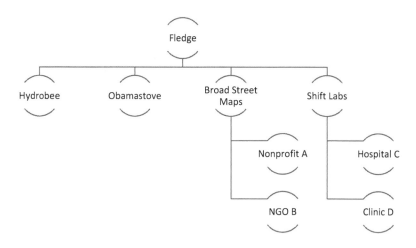

Indirect and doubly indirect impact of Fledge

That pattern is again repeated with Impact Hub Seattle, or any of the Impact Hubs around the world. Each of those organizations is a co-working and community space for impactful organization. Creating and curating the Impact Hub community helps impactful organizations succeed at their work. But in regards to the Impact Hub, their impact is all indirect, through their member organizations.

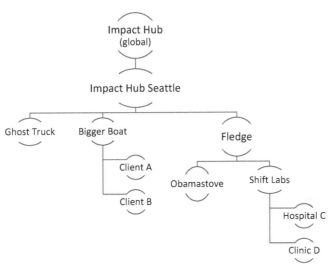

Multiple levels of indirection for Impact Hub Seattle

And like in the Fledge example, some members of the Hub are suppliers or service providers to charities, foundations, and impactful for-profits, making Impact Hub two or more levels of indirection away from the final impact.   Or more, as Fledge itself is a member of Impact Hub Seattle, and thus our indirection is always one step further away for Impact Hub Seattle, and two steps away from the greater Impact Hub global co-op.

0.01%, 1%, 10%, 50%, 100% (Reprise)

To help us measure the achieved impact taking into account indirection, we will once again use the restricted set of percentages that were introduced in CHAPTER 12.

This time, you pick the percentage that matches the contribution of the organization in question vs. the total all suppliers, vendors, and service provides which are used by the organization making the direct impact.

To measure the indirect, achieved impact, pick the largest of the following for the organization being measured:

- If the organization **has a direct impact** then measure **the full 100%** of the units
- If the organization is responsible for **50% or more** of the total intended impact, then measure **50%** of the units

  E.g., the project being measured is a 50:50 joint venture
- If the organization is responsible for **more than 10%** of the total intended impact, then measure **10%** of the units

  E.g. the organization is one of 10 or fewer suppliers to another impactful organization
- If the organization's efforts are **visible within the direct impact**, then measure **1%** of the units

  The intent is to spread the credit generously, if it is obvious where it originated from
- If the organization's efforts are **invisible within the final impact**, then measure the impact as **0.01%** of the units of the intended impact.

  Take some credit, but as always, don't be greedy in your measurements

Including this percentage will greatly reduce the measured impact for organizations which have indirect impact. However, this will reduce the overall amount of overcounting of impact when aggregating impact across multiple organizations, some of which may be suppliers to the same organization.

Let's look at an example to see how this plays out. Take two organizations: A is one of three major suppliers to B, which has a project with **50% of a P^1 complete**. What is the impact of A?

1. 50% of a P^1, = 500 units.
2. 10% of 500 units = 50 units.
3. Log (50) = 1.69
4. 1.69 ÷ 3 = 0.566
5. Indirect Impact = $P^{0.566}$

Let's look at another example. This time A is one of many service providers to C, with A's contribution clearly visible in the final impact. C has a project with **50% of a P¹ complete**. What is the impact of A?:

1. 50% of a P^1, = 500 units.
2. 1% of 500 units = 5 units.
3. Log (5) = 0.699
4. 0.699 ÷ 3 = 0.232
5. Indirect Impact = $P^{0.232}$

Given how this step further reduces the measurements, no doubt some organization will skip it to boost their scores. It is thus recommended that when reporting achieved impact, that the measurement be reported as including both indirect and direct impacts, to make it clear that this extra factor is taken into account.

For organizations where the impact is always indirect, four measurements can be reported: **potential, intended, achieved** (direct), and **achieved** (indirect). The achieved-direct measurement skips this adjustment, and the achieved-indirect includes it.

CHAPTER 18.
P^{n}ROI

With this single value of impact, we can turn back to the concept of SROI, and create an analogous P^{n}ROI. This is a ratio that ties impact to dollars.

P^{n}ROI is defined as the number of units per dollar of investment.

Note the ratio is units per dollar (Units/$), not index value per $. We could use the index value, but the logarithmic scale is not intuitive. Units are a nice, intuitive, linear scale, and thus easier to understand.

To convert an index back into a number of units (whole number or fraction), raise 1,000 to the power of the index value. You can do this with the x^y button on a scientific calculator, or using the POWER function in Excel. For example:

1. $P^1 = 1000^1 = 1,000$ units
2. $P^2 = 1000^2 = 1,000,000$ units
3. $P^{0.89} = 1,000^{0.89} = 470$ units
4. $P^{0.93} = 1,000^{0.93} = 610$ units
5. $P^{1.23} = 1,000^{1.23} = 5,000$ units
6. $P^{1.34} = 1,000^{1.34} = 10,500$ units

For negative index values, raise -1,000 to the negative of the index value:

7. $_{-1.06}P = -1,000^{1.06} = -1,490$ units
8. $_{-1.23}P = -1,000^{1.23} = -5,000$ units
9. $_{-1.34}P = -1,000^{1.34} = -10,500$ units

Mathematically, the positive and negative indexes are symmetric, hence the symmetry in examples 5 & 8 and 6 & 9. The other fractional values might look familiar; they are all taken from previous examples in the chapter on aggregating impact and net impact.

Once you have units, calculating P^nROI requires just one more division: divide those units by the number of dollars spent.

In this way, it is possible to compare the potential P^nROI of two hypothetical projects. For example, supposed **Project A is a potential P^2 and costs $1 million, and Project B is a potential P^3 costing $500 million.**

A. $P^2 \div \$1$ million = 1 million units $\div \$1$ million = 1 unit per dollar
B. $P^3 \div \$500$ million = 1 billion units $\div \$500$ million dollars = 2 units per dollar

Project B has twice the potential impact per dollar! Of course in real life, there are quite a few differences between funding and organizing a $1 million project and a $500 million project, but this ratio lets us see past those complexities and focus on the useful measure of the amount of impact per dollar of investment.

The P^nROI ratio works for fractional index values just as well as whole numbers. What is the P^nROI of a **$P^{1.23}$ at $10,000 vs. a $P^{1.34}$ at $12,000**?

A. $P^{1.23} \div \$10,000$ = 5,000 units $\div \$10,000$ = 0.50 units per dollar
B. $P^{1.34} \div \$12,000$ = 10,500 units $\div \$12,000$ = 0.875 units per dollar

Do be careful with the implied precision of these values, especially when working with the fractional index values. Remember, the values assigned to the intended impact span three orders of magnitude. One project may be 800 larger than another and yet receive the same index value. Plus, the percentages assigned to achieved impact are limited. One project with 40% completion and another with 10% completion are both counted as 10% complete. Those approximations can quickly wash away the differences between the small difference of 0.50 units and 0.85 units per dollar.

In general, what should a unit of impact cost? The index does not answer that question. A unit is not a person or a tree or a ton of carbon. A unit is a measure of progress. The P^nROI ratio allows you to use your computed measure of impact to compute **the cost per unit of impact**. Then you can compare that cost against the costs of other projects, and some day, benchmarks of similar projects.

CHAPTER 19.
More P²s, P³s, and P⁴s

Unlike the other measures of impact, the Pinchot Impact Index makes most impacts appear small and insignificant. Most impacts have a value of P^1, and in this index, it takes 1,000 fully-implemented P^1s to equal a single P^2.

That may seem counterproductive in a world that needs impactful solutions.

Perhaps that will prove to be true, but that is not my intent. What I like best about the tiny range of reasonable values in this index is that it showcases the possibilities for larger impacts.

I am an entrepreneur who spends every day working with early-stage mission-driven for-profit entrepreneurs who dream of making an impact in the world. The most common first conversation with these people is to question why they are pursuing an entrepreneurial path. Why are they starting their startup?

I tell all these entrepreneurs that their efforts will be all consuming. It will require all the time and energy they have. That there will be struggle and heartache in the future. That entrepreneurship is not an easy path. That when their friends and family tell them that they are crazy for doing it, that their friends and family are correct.

I also tell them that as long as they are heading down this chosen path, they might as well pick a big audacious goal, and aim to make a large impact on the world. The reality of startup life is that the small idea and the big idea will both consume all available time and resources. Both are unlikely to succeed. **So... if you are going to spend your time doing something, make it as big and impactful as possible**. If you succeed, then you'll have changed the world. If you fail, then hopefully you've made a little difference along the way.

I don't spend much time with nonprofit or government agencies, but I suspect the same advice applies there as well.

I want to live in a world with no hunger and no homelessness. I work in a neighborhood that is the center for both of those maladies of society in my home city, and see those issues most every day.

I want to see the end of the fossil fuel era in my lifetime. I want to continue travelling around the world, but do so on a supersonic plane powered by a renewable fuel. I want to take that plane to whichever city turns off the last coal powered electric generator.

I want my grandchildren to look at my funny when I talk about the common cold or the flu, just as I look at my grandparents funny when they talked about polio or smallpox or "consumption".

Have you ever tried to describe life without the Internet to a 10 year old? I can't wait for the day when a 10 year old shows me a technology that I don't understand. Perhaps a neural implant that controls the robot which cooks us dinner, then cleans the house, then truly connects the whole family together in ways that make Facebook look like a 19th century scrapbook.

And I want all of this not just for the most affluent 1% on the planet, but for everyone. A world where income equality is an old fashion idea found in history books, like dueling or phrenology or imperialism.

While the world described in P^6 may be out of reach in the next 200 years (Star Trek takes place in the 23rd Century), there is nothing stopping us from creating the worlds described as P^2, P^3, P^4, and P^5.

And as business and commerce are the most powerful forces on the planet today, I expect nearly all this impact to be created by companies. Companies doing good by doing good business.

CHAPTER 20.
Final Thoughts

The Pinchot Impact Index does not solve every problem of measuring, comparing, and aggregating impact, but it provides a valuable new tool in all three of those tasks.

For once, we have a universal measure of impact across any sector, which is useful for measuring, comparing, and aggregating potential, intended, and achieved impact.

It is a tool that works with both positive and negative impacts, including aggregating the two together.

And with this tool, we can finally compute a reasonable ratio of impact per dollar, without any of the issues of trying to measure impact itself in dollars.

Some of the potential issues of this index are covered in the Appendix, but none of those seem like insurmountable problems. All in all, this new index seems to be the breakthrough idea that impactful organizations have been waiting for.

APPENDIX

Additional thoughts and issues,
plus a bibliography, biography, and index

CHAPTER 21.
Objections

By this point, I suspect that many of the readers of this book will be questioning some or all of the choices in designing the index. This chapter provides some justifications for the most common objections.

1,000 is arbitrary

Why do the values go up by 1,000 times? Isn't that an arbitrary choice?

Yes, it is indeed arbitrary, but upon reflection, it seems the right choice. Here is why:

First and foremost, powers of ten make the mathematics easier. We can multiply by 100 and 1,000 and 1,000,000 far quicker and easier than multiplying by 2 or 3 or 15. Quick, name the first seven powers of 15. (I created a spreadsheet to tell me the answer: 15, 225, 3,375, 50,625, 759,375, 11,390,625, and 170,859,375.)

Second, scaling by a factor of 10 does not feel big enough. Such a scale would make a P^3 only 10 times more impactful than a P^2 and 100 times more impactful than a P^1. A P^3 is the end of homelessness or a pill that cures your cold. The difference in impact feels a lot more than 100 times larger than installing a solar panel on one building. 1,000,000 times feels more reasonable. That then makes for a factor of 1,000 per level.

Third, looking at the whole scale in units as well as values helps put this "feel" into perspective. At 10 times per level, P^1 is 10 units, P^2 is 100 units, ... upward to P^7 at 10,000,000 units. That makes a Star Trek's peace on Earth and end of hunger and poverty at P^6 just 1,000,000 times "better" than doing nothing. Again, that feels far too small. 1,000 times per level better captures the large differences. At 1,000 times per level, P^7 equals 10^{21} units a.k.a.

1,000,000,000,000,000,000,000 units. That big number made this scale feel sufficiently large to cover the gamut of possible impacts. (Note, to put 10^{21} in perspective, that number is about 1,000 times the 10^{18} sand grains on all the beaches on Earth. There are roughly 10^{18} number of grains of sand on Earth, and 10^{21} is 1,000 times bigger than 10^{18}. *(See hawaii.edu/suremath/jsand.html)*

Forth, I liked the fact that English has a name for each three orders of magnitude. Hundreds, thousands, millions, billion, trillions, etc. (in American English). That seemed quite a lot simpler than dealing with a factor of 100, where the levels are 100, 10,000, 1,000,000, 100,000,000, and 10,000,000,000. Ten thousand and 10 billion seem out of place in that sequence, despite each value being 100 times the previous value.

Fifth and finally, the scale of 1,000 times per level allowed the calculations for achieved impact to be simple and almost natural. The only issue was that achieving 1% of a P^n is valued as more units than completing a whole P^{n-1}. That is why 0.01% appears in the achieved impact measurement rule. With that tiny percentage 0.01% of 1,000,000 is 100, which not coincidentally is 10% of 1,000. The other percentages in the measurement rule (1%, 10%, 50%, 100%) are simple, natural measures of progress, and the factor of 1,000 lets us use those values with just the one small additional of 0.01%.

Having a scale and underlying units is confusing

Isn't it confusing to have values P^n and also numbers of units?

Agreed, it is more complex than other measurement scales. And agreed, when trying to describe this index, it can be troublesome to ensure the distinction between values as P^n and number of units.

That said, I could not pass up the benefits and simplicity of having the 0-7 scale. That was the big breakthrough idea in the midst of the conversation about the *Happo Dammo Ratio* with Gifford. We were trying to justify which damage was larger, a manicured golf course or a chlorinated swimming pool. The answer was to step out of the trees of specific values and up to the forest of orders of magnitude.

Limiting the choices of value to 7 solves so many problems and avoids almost every argument about comparing impacts. The limited scale led to a need to justify the range as logarithmic. The logarithmic nature then led to the need for some underlying units so that the values could be aggregated.

Or more simply, given the decision to limit the values to 0-7, the only way to make the index work for all three tasks of measuring, comparing, and aggregating impact was to include both the value and the underlying units.

Units have no units

The underlying units are not dollars or lives or happiness or any other measurable unit. They are unitless units. What are they?

Fundamentally, the units exist primarily to allow achieved impact to be measured, so that impact values can be aggregated. Given that, for achieved impacts, they can be thought of as progress.

Progress has no unit of measure other than percentage completion.

Progress is not equal to effort, as sometimes projects progress quite quickly, and at other times they get stuck, despite a lot of effort. Neither is progress equal to dollars, as more resources and more labor do not always produce more results. Nor is progress equal to time, as the oft-quoted fact says, nine women can not make a baby in one month.[4]

Since the units are progress, that allows us to talk about "the value of a completed P^n" or "five 10% completed P^ns", which is how I've described those values when aggregating values.

---

[4] From *The Mythical Man Month*, Fred Brooks

The measure is immeasurable

The values seem to be based on subjective feel more than data, no?

Yes, that is how they are described in this book. Subjective feel, and comparisons with the descriptions of the P values are how I expect other people to choose their values. There is today no objective way to collect data from the field or from market research to determine empirically whether an impact should be valued P^1 or P^2 or P^3 (or similarly $_{-1}P$ or $_{-2}P$ or $_{-3}P$).

This is indeed an unsolved problem. However, given the limited set of choices, and the rules of thumb provided in CHAPTER 11, my expectation is that most people will agree on where each impact falls on the index scale. 99% of projects have potential and intended impacts of P^1 and 99.9% of the time of either P^1 or P^2. A P^3 is by definition a million times larger than a P^1. I've been pitched thousands of impactful businesses, and only one I thought feasible comes even close to being a P^3 (see CHAPTER 28).

With that rule of thumb in mind, the question of measuring impact can be thought of as a simpler question, "Is this impact something extraordinary, a planet-scale systemic change?" If yes, P^2. If no, P^1. (Remember RULE 8: When it comes to to assigning, don't be greedy.)

The more troublesome part of this objection is in the measurement of achieved impact. In choosing between 0.01%, 1%, 10%, 50% and 100%. The intent of limiting these values is again to make such choices simpler and more obvious.

The gap between 1% and 10% is there on purpose, to make people think twice about claiming much progress. However, even if they do jump too soon to 10%, on the logarithmic scale, the difference between 10 points (1%) and 100 points (10%) is small. Thus some early claims of progress will not significantly change the index value, especially if aggregated across multiple projects or within a portfolio of organizations.

The gap between 10% and 50% in the measuring rule is again there on purpose, with no intermediate choices. This ensures that a meaningful amount of progress has been achieved before the next milestone of units is claimed. Similarly with no choice of other milestones before the 100% fully intended impact is achieved.

Or in short, the objections is valid, but overcome by the core concept of limited, logarithmic choices.

Everything is a P^1

If every value is a P^1, there isn't much to compare!

This is quite a powerful objection to the index. Yes, I do expect that 99% of impacts will be a P^1. I've said that directly in the previous section.

None the less, for small organizations, I don't see that as any worse than today's status quo, where they have no other comparable measure.

For medium-size organizations this index provides a way to calculate the aggregate of potential, intended and achieved impacts. Given any two projects, those values will no longer be a whole, round P^1, but instead fractional values.

And for large organizations, investment funds, and industry associations, the aggregation across multiple organizations creates a value that tells far more of a story than saying we work with 33 P^1's.

Subjectivity of values

Will two teams in two separate rooms always agree to the same values? Or in other words, is the measure purely subjective?

The index is designed to minimize disagreement by having such big differences between each P value. I expect that 99 out of 100 times, measures from different groups will be identical, and in that one occasion, the difference will be a P^2 vs. a P^1.

CHAPTER 28 includes a sample portfolio, with potential and intended impacts for each of 33 companies. Only one of those 33 has an intended impact of P^3. All others are P^1 or P^2. It is certainly possible that other people would measure that one P^3 as a P^2, but I would be incredibly surprised to see anyone claim any of those 33 companies deserves a value of P^4.

If differences do arise, I expect those differences will be in the measurement of the potential impacts, rather than the intended or achieved impacts.

The intent of measuring *potential* impact is so that we can quantify the level of impact if the problem being addressed were completely solved, 100%, worldwide. This is useful as it allows us to consider whether the problem we are tackling is itself truly important, separately from the specifics and limitations of our own solution and resources. I suspect that when measuring potential value, some people might get caught up in the specifics of the organization in question and their ability to scale to provide a global solution instead of solely on the problem itself.

In business planning, there is an analogous measure called the Total Addressable Market (TAM). That measure aims to quantify (in dollars) the size of the opportunity for the company and all its current and future competitors. It is a useful measure to understand how large a company might grow to be.

Comparing problems to the scale of homelessness and hunger (a P^2 and P^3) can be difficult and ultimately subjective. So yes, measuring potential impacts has some subjectivity to it. But since very few organizations intend to completely solve a global problem by themselves, that subjectivity falls away, because the only reasonable assignment remaining is P^1.

And yes, 0.0001% of the time, when you are measuring the impact of the organization which claims to have a working, affordable fusion reactor, then the potential impact might indeed merit a P^4. The subjective question then turns to whether that organization intends to replace 100% of the coal, gas, and oil burning electric generators (a P^4) or 1/1,000th of those generators (a P^3) or just a few before "selling out" (a P^2).

May the factor of 1,000 be with you!

CHAPTER 22.
Utopia & Symmetry

Given the horrors of $_{-7}P$ and the wonders of P^7, a scale from $_{-6}P$ through P^6 seems sufficient.

It probably is. However, that isn't really where the scale ends, is it? It costs us nothing to include the end of the universe and the awakening of all mankind, and it helps in understanding the scale, and thus they are included.

The key novelty to this index is the limited choices of values. My first draft included just eleven values, $_{-5}X$ though X^5, where $_{-5}X$ was the extinction of life in the universe and X^5 was the utopian good day on Star Trek. There were three problems with that smaller scale. (I'm using X^n instead of P^n to make it clear when I'm using the values from the first draft index.)

First, there wasn't enough space on the positive side. Solving homelessness and hunger were a single value. Those are both big issues, but feeding everyone on the planet seems more than 1,000 harder and more important than housing everyone. Housing, when solved, is solved for years. Meanwhile, serving two meals per day for a single year requires serving 730 meals, every day, without fail. Living without housing is hard. Living without food is impossible.

Second, given X^5 was free and unlimited access to whatever you need, X^4 was world peace, X^3 was the end of poverty, homelessness and hunger were both X^2. That left everything else smaller than those problems as a X^1. On the positive side, it means just about every positive impact was a X^1. However, it also meant that completing any 1,000 simple projects was equal to solving global homelessness and hunger. That gave far too much credit to the small projects.

Third, the index was not symmetric. It would be nice to have an X^5 replicator, but that was not anywhere near as nice as preventing the

$_{-5}X$ end of all life on Earth or end of the universe. The P^7 of enlightenment is there to try to create that symmetry.

Spreading the values of the index from $_{-7}P$ through P^7 solved all of these issues.

It made room to move solving world hunger up to P^3, making that equal to completing 1 million smaller impacts. That seems reasonable.

It spread homelessness, hunger, poverty, and world peace across separate levels, which seems like a logical progression.

And it opened up space at the bottom of the scale, allowing more possibilities for both P^1s and P^2s. This then led to the distinction (outlined in the rules of CHAPTER 11) that P^1s are impacts that help individuals compared to P^2s, which make systemic changes.

Adding any more levels would start us down the slippery slope of choices, no doubt introducing more arguments about Z^1s, Z^2s, and Z^3s. Thus fifteen (seven positive, seven negative, and zero) seems to be the right compromise between too many and too few levels in this index.

CHAPTER 23.
The Choice of P^n

Why is the value P^2 denoted as P^2 instead of P2 or $_p2$ or 2_p or 2^P or 2P or simply 2? The choice of P^2 as the notation makes the "P" prominent and the number tiny, and that seems counter-productive for a numeric measurement.

This is a good question and a reasonable objection to the chosen notation. I looked at all the options, and chose P^n for a few reasons.

First and foremost, the value stands out as something different and noteworthy. P^n does not look like an ordinary, everyday number. Most of us are not used to seeing capital letters with superscripts.

That distinctiveness of form makes it clear that the value is not an ordinary number, and if this measure becomes commonplace, it makes using the index far simpler, since the unique form stands out on a page of other numbers.

Second, the chosen form is similar in form to exponents in mathematics. The value P^n for values 0-7 is equal to 10^{3n} units. Mathematicians successfully handle pages of values full of exponents, despite their diminutive size.

That said, the values in this index do not exactly follow the form for exponents. The form shifts to $_{-n}P$ for values -1 through -7. I made that choice deliberately, from years of training as a undergraduate working on a degree in mathematics, where misplaced negative signs were common and devious typos. Having the negative values on the left and a subscript makes the negative sign almost redundant, and harder to be introduced accidentally as a typo.

Similarly, the value of zero is P_0, with the subscript zero to make it distinct from both the positive and negative values. This value, given it is limited to exactly nothing, may never be seen in practice, but none the less I wanted it to stand out.

Third, the chosen form works well with the fractional, aggregate values. In the value $P^{0.123}$, for example, the number 0.123 stands out more than when written as P0.123.

To my eye, the P in P0.123 resembles a currency symbol, like $0.123 or €0.123, but with a symbol that blends into the number rather a clear indication defining the type of units.

In the format $P^{0.123}$, the P and 0.123 are always distinct from each other, less easily confused, with the number resembling a decimal value, and with the whole value less likely to be misunderstood.

Fourth, of all the choices, P^n did the best job of reminding the reader that the scale is not linear. Most of the scales and measures we use every day are linear, and I wanted to best ensure that no one aggregated 1P + 1P + 1P as 3P, or P2 + P2 + P2 as 6P. The aggregate of three P^1s is equals to $P^{1.16}$, which is not a number obvious from staring at three 1's. Three P^2s is equal to $P^{2.16}$, three P^3s equal to $P^{3.16}$, which form a mathematical pattern that after a while starts to make sense.

Fifth and finally, I did give some thought to using a fancy P or a π (a Greek pi) or shrinking down the stylized P from the Pinchot University logo.

Using π, the form could be -5π through $\pi5$ without the subscripts or superscripts. However, that would no doubt lead to people multiplying by 3.14159, or raising 3.14159 exponentially or otherwise confusing the standards with the common mathematical value of pi.

Plus, I thought the standard P would be far easier to include in text files, spreadsheets, presentations, and web pages. Not every font contains a fancy P or symbol for π.

In the end, the choice of $_{-n}P$ and P^n seemed the best balance of form and function, with a dash of distinctiveness.

The Values are Too Small

Talking about P^1 and P^2 and especially $P^{0.699}$ make the impact seem miniscule. Wouldn't it be better to multiply all those values by 1000 and make those values $P^{1,000}$ and $P^{2,000}$ and P^{699}.

One of the goals of this index is to inspire people to do more, and yes, naming some progress 699 sounds like more than 0.699. However, multiplying the values by 100 or 1,000 doesn't fundamentally change the index, but does add an extra layer of complexity in converting between values and units.

This objection is analogous to saying that we should replace all dollars with a new currency that is 100 times larger, so that we replace $10 with §0.10, because §0.10 feels a lot less expensive.

Or if you have ever traveled to Japan, where US$1 is worth about ¥100, a ¥1,000 meal is a reasonably low price, as is a $10 American take-out bill. The numbers are 100 times different, but the values identical.

The point is that the scale of numbers within a currency system or any other measurement system is a feature that we get used to with use.

The direct conversion of P^n to 10^{3n} units is simple, and in my opinion not worth making more complicated.

CHAPTER 24.
We Still Need IRIS

The Pinchot Impact Index is not intended to replace the need for IRIS. The Pinchot Index is far too course-grained to measure the achieved impacts that are measured by the IRIS metrics.

Picking a simple example (three related metrics with uncommonly short descriptions), IRIS includes details such as:

PI4127
Trees Planted
Hectares of trees planted by the organization during the reporting period.

PI3848
Trees Planted: Native Species
Hectares of native species planted by the organization during the reporting period.

PI4907
Land Reforested
Hectares of land that have been reforested by the organization during the reporting period.

Metrics like these, and the other 488 in the current catalog are very useful in the day-to-day operations and management of impactful projects and organization.

It is nice to know that an achieved impact is $P^{1.34}$ on the Pinchot scale, but it is just as important to know that 30 hectares of trees were planted last quarter, up from 20 hectares the previous quarter, with a total goal of 500 hectares.

In management theory, the rule is, "you can't manage what you have not measured". IRIS provides 488 choices of standardized metrics for those measurements.

For more information on the IRIS standards, visit **iris.thegiin.org**.

CHAPTER 25.

We Still Need GIIRS & B Corporations

The Pinchot Impact Index does not replace the need for GIIRS investment ratings or Certified B Corporations. The B Impact Assessment underlying both these ratings provides a curated checklist of actions that companies can choose from, in order to improve their governance, improve the relations with vendors and other community members, and improve the environment. No company is expected to do everything on the list, but all companies will find something more to strive for from this list.

For example, the three questions from the Community section of the assessment seen below ask about whether a company picks vendors based on their social and environmental impact, and if so, by what criteria those decisions are made.

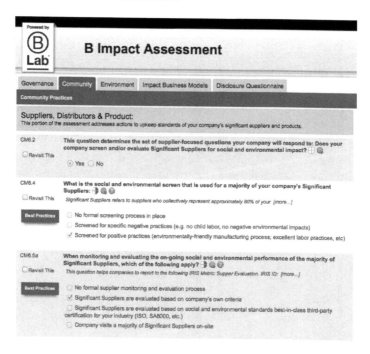

The Environment section is similar, as seen below with two very different questions, one on LEED certification, and the other on the specific types of recycling collected in the companies office(s).

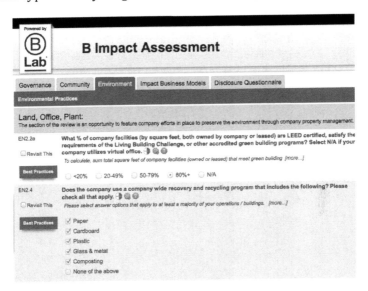

If you've not assessed your own company, try it today at *bimpactassessment.net.*

CHAPTER 26.
PwC's TIMM Language

PricewaterhouseCoopers (PwC) has created a what they call a new language for business decisions, the Total Impact Measurement and Management (TIMM) framework.

In the words of Professor Mervyn King SC, Chairman of the International Integrated Reporting Council:

"We know that today some 80% of the market capitalisation of companies is represented by so-called intangible assets which would not, according to financial reporting standards, be included as additives in a balance sheet.

While at the core of a business's performance is its financial return, because we report in monetary terms, a board has to take account of the legitimate and reasonable needs, interests and expectations of all its stakeholders and the resources used by the company.

Whilst it is clear that there are inputs other than the financial and manufactured resources such as human, intellectual, natural and social, the output or product and service of a company in turn has an impact on its stakeholders and the resources used by the company.

Integrated thinking requires all these factors to be considered in a holistic manner, such that a company can understand, and make decisions based on, the overall impact it has on all its stakeholders and generally on society, the environment and the economy.

I am delighted that PwC has developed the Total Impact Measurement and Management (TIMM) framework which demonstrates it is possible to carry out an impact study that puts a value on all a company's activities (or its product or service)."

This quote is from the opening of PwC's 2013 report *"Measuring and managing a total impact: A new language for business decisions"*
pwc.com/totalimpact

The key idea in TIMM is to measure all the impacts, positive and negative, within a project, plotting those results on a single graph. Multiple options can then be viewed side by side, to help make decisions that effect both the fiscal bottom line and net impact.

And example of one such graph is below, taken from the above-mentioned 2013 report. Note that green is positive and red negative.

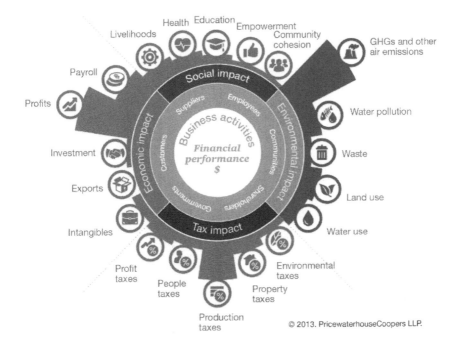

© 2013. PricewaterhouseCoopers LLP.

What is interesting about this approach is the breakdown of impact across four sectors, plus the further breakdown of those impact into five sub-categories.

The framework does not attempt to aggregate the results into a single measure. However, in order to generate a graph like this, there must be some units within each of the twenty categories.

If each of those measures were instead computed in units on the Pinchot scale, it becomes possible to aggregate this graph into a single value.

It is exciting to imagine the results of such a merger of frameworks, providing not only a means to measure, compare, and aggregate impact, but to also provide a visual means of breaking down that impact into common sub-components.

The open question then is whether the 20 categories chosen by PwC are sufficiently universal to make such a merged framework workable, or whether that would then lead to the same limitation seen in the Triple Bottom Line?

CHAPTER 27.

Other Limited Scales

One of the differentiating aspects of the Pinchot Impact Index is the use of a compressed scale, limited to just 0-7. While such a scale is not found in any of the other major impact measurement systems, such limited scales are far from uncommon. They are in fact successfully used by millions of people daily on a variety of online services.

Two of those most popular scales range from 1-5. One is the Amazon rating system:

The other is the Netflix rating system, which doubles as a predictive measure of how much you'll like the movie:

In both of these, your choices are limited to 1, 2, 3, 4 or 5 stars, and in the case of Netflix, they limit the display of their predictions to ¼, ½, ¾ and full stars.

Netflix tells its customer what each number of stars means:

- 1 star = "Hated It"
- 2 stars = "Didn't like It"
- 3 stars = "Liked It"
- 4 stars = "Really Liked It"
- 5 stars = "Loved It".

Amazon does not do this, but in practice, the Amazon stars seem to have similar meanings. Given this spread of ratings, note that this is somewhat analogous to the full span of values in the Pinchot index, as 1 and 2 stars at Netflix and Amazon are negative ratings.

Anecdotally, it certainly seems like most customers use this scale as if it were logarithmic, saving the five star ratings for only the small few items that stand out in quality. And similarly saving the one star ratings for movies and items that greatly disappointed.

Thus, the difference between a 1 and 2 or 4 and 5 is much larger than the difference between a 2 and 3 or 3 and 4. That is a logarithmic scale.

Here's how you can use any experience at Netflix and Amazon to help you measure impact...

Most impactful organizations today are "less bad" solutions (i.e. doing less damage than the status quo), which is a $_{-1}P$ on the Pinchot scale, equivalent to three stars at Amazon or Netflix. Nearly all positive impacts you encounter will be a P^1, equivalent to four stars. Save the rare, huge P^2 impacts for five stars. And if you are lucky enough to work on a P^3, then think about that as ten stars, so big as to break the whole star rating system.

The world needs a few blockbuster impacts more than it needs blockbuster movies!

CHAPTER 28.

Example Ratings / Sample Portfolio

To provide some real life examples, let's take a look at the Fledge portfolio of graduate *fledglings*. These are all mission-driven for-profit companies, each with an intended impact.

This, not coincidentally, is the portfolio of companies I've worked with between 2012 and 2014 while running Fledge, the conscious company accelerator. I thus know these companies well. Well enough to accurately assess their potential, intended, and achieved impacts. Plus they are all small enough that each has just a single project to track.

As of the end of 2014, the portfolio contained 33 companies:

 Evrnu has created a process that recycles cotton. Today, tens of millions of tons of cotton garments are sent to the landfill, replaced with tens of millions of tons of new fabric grown from the ground. With Evrnu, this linear process of waste will become a circular, sustainable system. evrnu.com

Potential impact: P^3 Intended impact: P^2

Broad Street Maps works with global health organizations, turning static spreadsheets into dynamic maps in order to better understand the social and geographic determinants of health, and ultimately improve the delivery of care and planning efforts. broadstreetmaps.com

Potential impact: P^2 Intended impact: P^1

BURN Manufacturing was created to address the enormous need for clean cook stoves in the developing world where 2 million people die each year from indoor cooking smoke. BURN plans on manufacturing millions of high efficiency cook stoves in Africa that will impact the lives of tens of millions of people, and save more than 120 million trees. burnmanufacturing.com

Potential impact: P² Intended impact: P¹

 Close to Home is an marketplace for post-disaster, temporary homes. A place to go when FEMA lets you down, or for less massive disasters, such as home fires or remodels. Close to Home allows communities to remain in place after disasters, rather than creating weather refugees, who often never return home. c2hh.com

Potential impact: P² Intended impact: P¹

 Community Sourced Capital provides a simple way for community members to lend money to the local businesses where they find the most value. By turning stakeholders into invested business supporters, CSC creates stronger customer/business relationships, and in doing so, strengthens the local economy. communitysourcedcapital.com

Potential impact: P² Intended impact: P¹

 Deehubs takes social media out into the streets, expanding free speech beyond the confines of phones, tablets, and computers, creating public stages everyone to (briefly) share their thoughts, dreams, and visions of a better future. deehubs.com

Potential impact: P² Intended impact: P¹

Ecosawa aims to hoist Kenya out of poverty through an entrepreneurship training program, distributed throughout all the rural communities across the country, then repeating the process across the rest of Africa. ecosawa.com

Potential impact: P² Intended impact: P¹

 Obamastove manufactures and distributes affordable, efficient cookstoves throughout Ethiopia, ridding homes of smoke, halving the use of fuel, improving the lives of millions in the daily chore of cooking. obamastove.com

Potential impact: P² Intended impact: P¹

 Shift Labs brings high-impact, life-improving technologies to bottom of the pyramid medical practitioners and institutions. shiftlabs.com

Potential impact: P² Intended impact: P¹

 Simpolfy brings transparency and insights of American politics to voters, creating "report cards" for representatives, helping voters know who best represents their views, and holding representatives accountable to their constituents. simpolfy.com

Potential impact: P² Intended impact: P¹

Stockbox Neighborhood Grocery is rolling out a network of stores that are the hub for fresh food, community connections, engaging experiences, and innovation in grocery, especially in those communities which today lack access to fresh, healthy food. stockboxgrocers.com

Potential impact: P² Intended impact: P¹

Tansa Clean is cleaning the rivers, lakes, and fields of India, redirecting the stream of human waste into the existing "fleet" of biodigestors, turning what would be harmful waste into clean energy and pathogen-free fertilizer. tansaclean.com

Potential impact: P² Intended impact: P¹

 UbrLocal is a marketplace for urban grown food and home manufactured food products. It's like a farmer's market, but available 24/7 online. ubrlocal.com

Potential impact: P² Intended impact: P¹

 Activate Hub allows you to discover events, organizations and people impacting your community. activatehub.org

Potential impact: P¹ Intended impact: P¹

 AlchemList is an online wish list for non-profits. It's like Craigstlist or Freecycle, but where you know your stuff is going to a cause you care about. alchemlist.org

Potential impact: P¹ Intended impact: P¹

DISTRIBUTED ENERGY MANAGEMENT **Distributed Energy Management** helps business owners save money on their utility bills, by managing their total utility budget. This unique financial structure creates a painless way to invest in energy conservation. de-mgmt.com

Potential impact: P¹ Intended impact: P¹

East Africa Fruit *is bringing the best-practices of modern fruit and vegetable farming to Tanzania. EA Fruit aggregates and distributes produce from local farmers (over 50 as of 2014) working to increase the quality from these farms while simultaneously increasing their income well above the national average. eafruitsfarm.com*

Potential impact: P¹ Intended impact: P¹

HERE builds technology to create stronger, safer, and more resilient communities in cities across the world. here-inc.com

Potential impact: P¹ Intended impact: P¹

 HydroBee has created a handheld, turbine rechargable battery to power USB devices such as phones, tablets, and LED lights. hydrobee.com

Potential impact: P¹ Intended impact: P¹

Juabar creates profitable energy franchises by investing in Tanzanian entrepreneurs (Juapreneurs) to bring solar recharging kiosks to their communities. juabar.com

Potential impact: P¹ Intended impact: P¹

Karibu Solar designs and manufactures affordable modular solar "business in a box" for African entrepreneurs who sell solar daily at the price of kerosene. karibusolar.com

Potential impact: P¹ Intended impact: P¹

Kodeza engages communities in how to best direct funding and resources so that they have a sustained impact, lessening the burden of project planning, while helping to create autonomy for the community. kodeza.com

Potential impact: P¹   Intended impact: P¹

Little Gray Farms is America's first and only snail farm, replacing the $300 million market of imported, canned escargot. littlegrayfarms.com

Potential impact: P¹   Intended impact: P¹

myTurn is the software infrastructure that enables rental shops to manage their inventory, put it all online, and make it as easy for consumers to rent, as it is to purchase. myturn.com

Potential impact: P¹   Intended impact: P¹

Personify.it is a location-centric application that lets you quickly find opportunities to volunteer your time anywhere you are using your mobile phone. personify.it

Potential impact: P¹   Intended impact: P¹

Self Spark helps people "hack" their lives to make them better. Like Startup Weekend for entrepreneurs, Self Spark helps people get on the path toward helping themselves. selfspark.com

Potential impact: P¹   Intended impact: P¹

Serve Smart is an online course that trains volunteers to serve with humility, vulnerability and empathy. It's perfect for service learning programs and other service centers that place volunteers domestically or abroad. serve-smart.com

Potential impact: P¹   Intended impact: P¹

The Seattle Good Business Network is an organization comprised of residents and local independent businesses that share a vision for a resilient, vibrant local economy – one that's rooted in local ownership, a healthy environment, and strong community. seattlenetwork.org

Potential impact: P¹ Intended impact: P¹

 Seeder is a marketplace of green building materials, helping building owners find great vendors and helping vendors find green builders. seeder.cc

Potential impact: P¹ Intended impact: P¹

 Snohomish Soap produces "authentically local" handmade soaps, manufactured by a distributed network of stay-at-home mothers and other disadvantaged women. snohomishsoapcompany.com

Potential impact: P¹ Intended impact: P¹

 TayaSola teaches people in Africa how to produce their own clean power and light, providing kits for solar lighting, cellphone charging, and more. tayasola.com

Potential impact: P¹ Intended impact: P¹

 Trash Backwards encourages reuse and upcycle solutions to combat the problem of excess stuff in our society. trashbackwards.com.
And beyond trash, the Trash Backwards team has launched the *Buy Nothing Project*, a community for sharing and giving the stuff we already have, but are not using. buynothingproject.org

Potential impact: P¹ Intended impact: P¹

Village Green builds capacity and community for conscious businesses through resource sharing. Events include the *Green Breakfast Club*, a series of events begun in New York City. villagegreen.is

Potential impact: P¹   Intended impact: P¹

Note that all the measures are P^1 or P^2 except for Evrnu, which has created a world-changing technology that makes cotton recyclable. This technology has the potential to eliminate 90% of all cotton farming on the planet, and with it, free up billions of gallons of fresh water for other uses, eliminate millions of gallons of pesticides and herbicides from the ecosystem, and prevent millions of tons of waste from the landfill each year.

Evrnu intends to be the catalyst that makes this change occur, but despite that intent, they are unlikely to achieve that goal alone. Thomas Edison and his company General Electric sparked the electrification of the world, but that one company did not sell even 1% of all light bulbs, electric generators, electrical grids, etc. Westinghouse, Siemens, Philips and tens of thousands of electric companies were involved in implementing the electrification process, which today still fails to reach over 1 billion citizens of the world.

This portfolio of 33 companies includes 13 companies with a *potential* impact of P^2 or P^3, but where none of those companies have a matching *intended* impact. In each of these cases, the companies have an intended impact one level lower than their potential impact. Remember the 80%/20% rule from CHAPTER 12, and remember, if you are not sure of the right value, don't be greedy with values.

Speaking of not being greedy, let's look at the rating of Ecosawa. The team at Ecosawa claims to have a cure for poverty. That said, the odds are small that they will manage to implement that change across all of Kenya, let alone impacting the 3+ billion people who live on $2/day or less. A solution to poverty is a P^4, 1,000 times larger in impact to Evernu's potential P^3. However, whereas Evrnu has a solution that may trigger the systemic change required to fulfill that P^3 impact, Ecosawa (and every other company in this portfolio tackling issues of poverty) has a solution that will at best make a noticeable change to the world. But even if copied by others, it is alone insufficient to eliminate poverty. Hence I've rated Ecosawa as a potential P^2 and an intended P^1.

Overall, this portfolio has a lot of potential. Far more than a random selection of mission-driven companies. These companies were specifically chosen from hundreds of applicants for their audacious potential. That said, only one third have a potential rating higher than P^1 and only one of the 33 has a P^2 rating for intended impact. Most of these companies, if they succeed, are likely to only make a local impact in solving their problems, and a local impact is typically less than 1% of a global solution.

None the less, these are companies not doing business as usual. They are making the world better than when they started. If nothing else, they will demonstrate to the world that it is possible for businesses to have a positive impact while doing business. Ideally, they will copied by others, to ultimately fulfill their potential impact.

Aggregating the total potential impact, we have 20 P^1s plus 12 P^2s, plus 1 P^3. That is 20,000 units plus 12,000,000 units plus 1,000,000,000 units, or a total of 1,012,020,000 units. Using the calculation explained in CHAPTER 14, the result is a $P^{3.002}$. The single P3 dominates the aggregation, as it is 1 million times larger than the P^1s and 1 thousand time larger than the P^2s. Without that lone P^3, the aggregate of the other 32 companies is $P^{2.36}$.

Aggregating the total intended impact, we have 32 P^1s plus 1 P^2. That is 32,000 units plus 1,000,000 units, or a total of 1,032,000 units, equal to a $P^{2.005}$. Again, the lone P^2 dominates the results. Without it, the other 32 companies aggregate to a is $P^{1.50}$.

The achieved impact is far more complicated to compute. We need to know the progress of each company, rated on the percentage scale of 0.01%, 1%, 10%, 50%, or 100%. Given the early-stage nature of all the fledglings, as of 2015 some are still at the 0% stage, some at the 0.01%, and a few at 1%. The most advanced is still a year or two away from reaching 10% or more of its intended impact.

Plus, when computing the aggregate achieved impact, we need to be clear about whether we are talking about the aggregate direct impact of the organizations being aggregated, or the indirect impact of the parent organization. In this case, let's start with the aggregate achieved impact of the portfolio itself.

To see what such an aggregating would look like let's simply take 0% for Envrnu (the only intended P^2), then 0.01% for 11 of the companies and 1% for the other 11 companies.

Aggregating those values, we get:

- 0.01% P^1 x 11 = 1 units x 11 = 11 units
- 1% P^1 x 11 = 10 units x 11 = 110 units
- Total of 121 units
- $P^{0.695}$

Given 121 units is only 12% of the 1,000 units equal to a complete P^1, it may seem surprising that the value of 121 units is $P^{0.695}$. That is due to the underlying logarithmic scale which grows at a different rate than a more intuitive, linear scale.

Lastly, we can compute the indirect impact of Fledge itself. Our program provides only a small seed investment, 10 weeks of intense training, plus some ongoing support. Without Fledge, some of the fledglings might never have existed, but even in those cases, we cannot claim to have provided more than 1% of the effort required to succeed.

To keep things simple, let's claim 1% of the impact across the whole portfolio. Using the rules from CHAPTER 17, we get:

- 121 total units of achieved impact (see the previous example)
- 1% of 121 = 1.21 units
- $P^{0.016}$

Now that looks like a tiny value, but accurately portray the facts at hand given Fledge's indirect level of impact, and the early stage of the fledglings. Proudly, the value is positive, and I have little doubt that this value will grow tremendously as the fledglings begin to achieve their intended impacts.

As demonstrated, this scale provides a method to produce four sets of aggregate values for our model portfolio. Values that we could compare to other portfolios, and values that we could use to calculate impact per dollars, or P^nROI as described in CHAPTER 18.

CHAPTER 29.

Log Log Scales

After reflecting on the range of potential impacts, I am more convinced that a log log scale better captures the vast scale of impact than just a log scale. However, using a log log scale is impractical so I will keep the Index scale as it is. But for those readers who are interested, I will explore the advantages of a log log scale here.

The 1,000 unit per level, seven level scale provides a range of 10^{21} values, but is Peace on Earth (a P^4) truly just a trillion times more impactful than volunteering an hour at the food bank (a P^1)? A trillion is a big number, but we have markets that trade a trillion dollars in a day. Perhaps we want a scale that grows even faster.

There is a name for this in mathematics: a log log scale.

For example:

- $LL^1 = 1$
- $LL^2 = 10$ (10x larger)
- $LL^3 = 1,000$ (100x larger)
- $LL^4 = 1,000,000$ (1,000x larger)
- $LL^5 = 1,000,000,000,000,000$ (1,000,000x larger)

These scales grow oodles faster than logarithmic scales. And the scale above grows so fast that the seventh level is too big to fathom. It very well could represent nirvana.

However, the problem is that log log scales are even less intuitive than log scales, especially when it comes to computing percentage completions. 1% of that LL^4 is 10,000, 10x the LL^3, but 1% of the LL^5 is 10,000,000,000,000, which is so large compared to the LL^4 that it might as well be equal to LL^5. In a log log scale, we'd need more complex rules for measuring achieved impacts, rather than using percentages, which we learned back in grammar school.

One fix may be to give up using factors of 10. There is nothing sacred about 10's. A log log scale using 2's would look like:

- $LL^1 = 1$
- $LL^2 = 2$ (2x larger)
- $LL^3 = 8$ (4x larger)
- $LL^4 = 128$ (16x larger)
- $LL^5 = 32,768$ (256x larger)
- $LL^6 = 2,147,483,648$ (65,536x larger)
- $LL^7 = 9.22 \times 10^{18}$ (4.29 billion times larger)

And a log log scale using 5's:

- $LL^1 = 1$
- $LL^2 = 5$ (5x larger)
- $LL^3 = 125$ (25x larger)
- $LL^4 = 78,125$ (625x larger)
- $LL^5 = 30,517,578,125$ (390,625x larger)
- $LL^6 = 4.66 \times 10^{21}$ (15.3 billion times larger)

These scales grow wickedly fast, but start out too slowly to help us differentiate values, and after the 4th or 5th level reach values that are as ludicrous to work with as the base 10 scale. Plus, few of us can look at a number like 2,147,483,648 and know that it is equal to 2^{31}.

Using a scale of 1,000 times between levels keeps the numbers nice and round, keeps the mathematics as simple as possible, and keeps the number of units within everyday values. Governments and businesses today deal with billions and trillions of dollars. We should thus have some grasp of what these numbers mean. (The quadrillions and quintillions can be ignored for now, until someone invents a replicator or finds a better way to teach meditation.)

Plus, in keeping with three orders of magnitude between levels, the 0.01%, 1%, 10% rules of measuring completeness of impact are simple arithmetic. In a log log scale, we would need something more log log-like than percentages. So we will set aside the log log scale, and stick to the "simpler" log scale.

CHAPTER 30.
Feedback & Conversations

The Pinchot Impact Index is not the be-all, end-all in measuring, comparing, and aggregating impact. It's unlikely to prove perfect by any measure.

You are invited to help make it better.

Bring your comments, questions, and ideas to **pinchotimpact.org**. Join the conversation to help iterate on this idea to make it more useful and more widely adopted.

Further Reading

Impact Measurement Standards

IRIS – iris.thegiin.org
GIIRS - giirs.org
SROI - thesroinetwork.org

PwC's *Total Impact Measurement and Management* -
pwc.com/totalimpact

Recommended books

The B Corp Handbook by Ryan Honeyman
The Business Solution to Poverty by Paul Polak and Mal Warwick
Evil Plans by Hugh MacLeod
The Monk and the Riddle by Randy Komisar
Owning Our Future by Marjorie Kelly
The Responsible Business by Carol Sanford
The Responsible Entrepreneur by Carol Sanford
If Kids Ran the World by Leo & Diane Dillon

Luni's books on entrepreneurship, available on Amazon.com:
The Next Step: Guiding you from idea to startup
The Next Step: A guide to startup sales and marketing
The Next Step: A guide to building a startup financial plan
The Next Step: A guide to pitching your idea
The Next Step: Realities of funding a startup
The Next Step: A guide to dividing equity
The Next Step: The Business Presentation Pyramid

Luni's books, lectures, and blog

Thoughts on impact, entrepreneurship and investing -
lunarmobiscuit.com/blog

Acknowledgements

Thank you to Gifford Pinchot III, Intrapreneur in Residence and co-founder of the Bainbridge Graduate Institute (bgi.pinchot.edu) for his foresight into the future of entrepreneurship, his openness to my mind's wanderings, and for inspiring this new measure of impact.

Thank you to the students, alumni, and staff at Pinchot University (pinchot.edu), who helped question, push, and poke this idea to get it into the form you have read today.

Thank you to the *fledglings* of Fledge, my conscious company accelerator (fledge.co), whose own impactful startups inspire me to do more good in the world.

And most of all, thanks to my brilliant wife and editor, Monica Aufrecht, who relentlessly ensured my words matched my thoughts, and more importantly, insisted I rewrite those words until they would be understandable to you without having a degree in mathematics or an MBA.

Her suggestions and edits increased the value of this book by at least an order of magnitude, if not three!

The beautiful cover image has been graciously provided by Andreas Levers
flickr.com/photos/96dpi/3287904733

About the Author

Michael "Luni" Libes is a 20+ year serial entrepreneur and founder of Fledge, the conscious company accelerator, helping entrepreneurs who aim to do good for the world, while simultaneously doing good business.
fledge.co @FledgeLLC

Luni is the creator and Global Managing Director of Kick, a pre-accelerator program providing business education and guidance to entrepreneurs globally, operating in numerous cities around the world.
kickincubator.com @KickIncubator

Luni is an Entrepreneur in Residence and Entrepreneurship Instructor at Pinchot, advisor to The Impact Hub Seattle, to SURF Incubator, and to a dozen startup companies. He is also an Entrepreneur in Residence Emeritus for the University of Washington's CoMotion center for impact and innovation.
bgi.pinchot.edu   comotion.uw.edu
thehubseattle.com   surfincubator.com

Luni began his 20+ year career in software, founding and co-founding four startups and joining a fifth. These include: Ground Truth (mobile market research and analysis), Medio Systems (mobile search and advertising), Mforma (mobile gaming and applications), 2WAY (enterprise collaboration systems), and Nimble (pen computing, PDAs, and early smartphones).

This book, Luni's Next Step series of books on entrepreneurship, and his blog can be found at lunarmobiscuit.com. *@Lunarmobiscuit*

Index

8

80/20 Rule, 55

A

achieved impact, 17, 51, 53, 68

B

B Analytics, 12, 22
B Corporation, 12, 92
B Impact Assessment, 12, 14, 18, 20, 92
B Impact Report, 13
B Lab, 12
Bainbridge Graduate Institute, ii, iii, 8, 117
Be greedy and bold, 51, 72
BHAG, 44
big hairy audacious goals, 44
black swan, 47

C

common cold, 43
corporate governance, 4, 12, 22

D

doing good, 3
doing harm, 3
Don't be greedy, 51, 56, 82, 106
Double Bottom Line, 9

E

enlightenment, 39

Environmental, Social, and Corporate Governance, 4

F

famine, 47
Fledge, 15, 65, 99
flu, 43

G

Gifford Pinchot I, ii
Gifford Pinchot III, ii, iii, 38, 115
GIIN, 10
GIIRS, 12, 22, 92
Give Well, 16
Global Impact Investing Ratings System, 12
Global Impact Investors Network, 10

H

Happo Dammo Ratio, ii, iv, 79
homeless, 44
hunger, 42

I

impact
  achieved, 17, 51, 53, 68
  indirect, 65
  intended, 17, 51, 68
  net, 61
  potential, 17, 51, 68, 84
Impact Hub Seattle, 15, 65, 117
Impact Reporting & Investment Standards, 10
indirect impact, 65

intended impact, 17, 51, 68
IRIS, 10, 11, 18, 33, 91

L

logarithmic scale, 31, 38
logarithms, 29

N

net impact, 61
nuclear war, 47

O

orders of magnitude, 27, 33

P

pandemic, 47
Peace on Earth, 40
People, Planet, and Profits, 8
Pinchot University, ii, 38, 115
plague, 47
P^nROI, 69
potential impact, 17, 51, 68, 84
poverty, 42
POWER, 69

PricewaterhouseCoopers, 94
Public Benefit Corporation, 13

R

return on investment, 9
ROI, 9

S

sand grains, 79
scientific notation, 26
social return on investment, 9
SROI, 9, 17, 20, 21, 69
Star Trek, 40, 73
Sustainable Business, ii
systemic change, 44, 50
systemic damage, 46

T

The Mythical Man Month, 80
Total Addressable Market, 84
Triple Bottom Line, 8, 96

U

utopia, 39

18350289R00075

Made in the USA
Middletown, DE
02 March 2015